FIVE IN A ROW
VOLUME 1

BY
JANE CLAIRE LAMBERT

FIVE IN A ROW PUBLISHING · GRANDVIEW, MISSOURI

Five in a Row, Volume 1
Revised Second Edition

ISBN 1-888659-00-9

Copyright © 1994, 1997 by Jane Claire Lambert
Cover painting Copyright © 1997 by Five in a Row Publishing

Published by:
Five in a Row Publishing
P.O. Box 707
Grandview, MO 64030-0707
(816) 331-5769

Send all requests for information to the above address.

Original cover oil painting created for *Five in a Row* by:
Deborah Deonigi
P.O. Box 1140
Maple Valley, WA 98038
(206) 413-9118

Printed in the United States of America

To my Mother, whose pure love of literature is contagious.
To my Dad, who encouraged me to "read the good stuff."
And to my Husband...who reads to me.

Special thanks to the "Guinea Pigs" who first tried *Five in a Row*
Our daughters, Becky and Carrie
and our dear friends Caleb, Benjamin and Nate.

Table of Contents

Introduction

Good books have always been the doorway to learning. That doorway leads to growth and an appreciation for the wonders around us. Come along on a learning adventure using picture books to open the door to art, history, vocabulary, geography, science, human relationships, math and writing!

No matter how young, children get a substantial educational head-start from books, and *Five in a Row* has been created to bring excitement and fun to learning and to enrich children's lives. These lesson plans are simple in concept, but rich in results. Read the chosen book in its entirety *each day for at least a week.* After each reading, choose an exercise to share with your student, and watch their world expand as you begin to show them facets of the story they would never have recognized without your purposeful guidance. As a teacher of this material, you will find that you become excited and interested in a variety of subjects too. You'll rediscover the joy of learning and you'll build a special bond between you and your student as the two of you go on a learning adventure together.

This curriculum is intended to be extremely flexible, allowing you the option to do any or all of the exercises for each story. You may elect to skip over certain exercises which do not fit the needs of your student and you may place additional emphasis on certain exercises which seem appropriate. You will find more exercises than you can use in a week, so enjoy choosing just the right lesson elements for your students.

You can adjust classroom time to fit your needs as well. By using only one lesson element each day, you can work through *Five in a Row* in as little as 30 minutes daily, including the time to read the book. If you choose to use all of the lesson elements, field trips and follow-up exercises, you could easily spend several hours daily. Use *Five in a Row* however it best suits your needs and the needs of your students.

The technique of reading the same story for at least five days in a row is one that I have tested in teaching for more than eight years. I continue to be amazed at the effectiveness of this technique! Each book will become very special to the children. They will remember more and more about the story, but more importantly, they will begin to think more critically (even four year olds!) as they begin wondering how certain portions of the story came to be, or how the characters solved a certain problem. These results could never be achieved in just one reading.

Students will see how the illustrator accomplished certain effects and they'll be encouraged to begin exploring those techniques in their own art. You'll see your students learning about science, math, and history by the things you bring to the discussion every day. Your students will have the opportunity to try new activities they read about, or to learn more about a variety of people, places or animals. You'll also discover them asking more questions than ever before. By the end of the week, a new book will have become their friend for life.

Perhaps the most valuable benefit of using *Five in a Row* is that the young students learn to completely critique a work (with your guidance), and that skill will serve them well as they learn to read for themselves. Your students will begin looking to see whether a book is a Caldecott or a Newberry medal winner. They'll quickly classify a new book as either fact or fiction. They'll be able to articulate the point of view from which the story has been written. They will know about a wide variety of literary techniques and learn to recognize them for themselves.You'll be delighted when your students begin to evaluate the illustrator's medium and technique.

All of this is imparted in a fun learning environment. Students think you're just reading them a book, but they're learning so much every day! The more lessons you do together, the more skills your young students will acquire; skills which will benefit them through high school, college and throughout life!

Welcome to the wonderful world of *Five in a Row*. You are the leader for this adventure, so gather the children around you and have a great time!

Jane Claire Lambert
May, 1994

*"The goal of our instruction is to lead children to fall in love
with good books and and to embrace the joy of learning."*

About the Books Themselves

Sutherland and Arbuthnot write in <u>Children and Books</u>, *"Aesthetic satisfaction
comes to small children as well as to adults, and the development of their taste depends not
only on their initial capacities but also on <u>the material they encounter and the way in
which it is presented.</u>"** (emphasis added)

If you're like most of us, you can directly attribute a lifelong interest in at least one
topic to the quality and creativity with which some particular teacher or a parent introduced the subject to you as a child. Likewise, you may well have nurtured a lifelong dis-
taste for certain subjects for the same reason; an unpleasant early experience.

Sutherland and Arbuthnot go on to suggest that by selecting excellent children's literature and reading it together each day, children have the opportunity to *"catch a new
theme, savor the beauty, the subtle humor or a special meaning that eluded them at first."*

"Sometimes," the authors suggest, *"an adult has the privilege of seeing this discovery take place. The children's faces come suddenly alive; their eyes shine. They may be
anticipating an amusing conclusion or a heroic triumph. There is a sudden chuckle or
breath is exhaled like a sigh. The book has moved them, perhaps even to laughter or tears,
in any case there is a deep inner satisfaction and they will turn to books again with antici-
pation."*

Sutherland and Arbuthnot conclude, *"Once they have experienced the joy of reading
they have acquired a habit that will serve them all their lives. It is important, therefore,
that those who guide their reading select wisely."*

It is within this context that the titles for *Five in a Row* have been chosen. In each
case content was of supreme importance. Books were chosen that showcase close family
relationships, personal triumphs, and persevering in times of trial. There are books with

people characters and stories with animal characters, but in all the stories the characters touch the reader's heart and demonstrate life's truths. Please remember, however, that our selection of a particular title by an author does *not* mean that we endorse *everything* from that author. We're aware of several cases where authors have written marvelous books and very questionable books as well. Please take the time to review any book you bring home from the library *before* reading it to your children!

In addition to content, the books also cover a wide range of artistic expression: from the beautiful portraiture of Allen Say to the hilarious pictures of Marjorie Priceman; from the warm homey drawings of Robert McCloskey to the action-packed illustrations of Virginia Lee Burton. Each title was selected for its magnificent art, beautifully rendered for the utter appreciation and enjoyment of children. Art to appreciate; art to learn from and art to be remembered for a lifetime!

It has been said some stories must be talked over or listened to while *someone who knows and loves them* reads aloud.* (emphasis added) If *you* come to love the stories your student will too.

With these standards in mind we hope you and your student find a special place in your heart for these stories and for the concept of *Five in a Row.*

*Sutherland and Arbuthnot, *Children and Books,* Harper Collins Publishers, 8th ed., 1991.

How to Use *Five In a Row*

Select a book to study with your student. There is no right or wrong order for covering the material, although in the Appendix, you'll find a suggested semester reading calendar for the fall term which links several stories to the appropriate seasons of the year.

Some teachers will choose to purchase each book as a valuable addition to their permanent library. Of course, any public library should have (or be able to request) each of the titles in this book. (See "Finding the Books" in the Appendix for more information.)

Important Note: *Please* take the time to read the book aloud to your student each day <u>before</u> covering the lesson material. *Five in a Row* was designed and tested to be read daily! The repetition is essential to your student's learning process, and the time you spend reading together is just as important as the lesson material itself.

In the Appendix, you will find a sample planning work sheet for *Who Owns the Sun?* You'll also find a blank work sheet which you can reproduce and use for each FIAR story you study. The sample sheet shows how to correlate the teacher's guide suggestions and plans to the five days of the week you will study each particular book. Or, feel free to design your own worksheet. Some teachers don't care to use planning sheets at all. They work directly from *Five in a Row* manual. Do whatever works for you!

Notice the sample lesson plan is outlined briefly and gives you a quick reference for the week. Not every lesson suggested in the Teacher's Guide under *Who Owns the Sun?* is listed on the sample lesson. This is because there are too many lessons in the teacher's manual for one week. So you may choose the ones that are especially suited to *your* student and list them on the blank planning sheet. The subjects Math, Science, Art, etc., do not have to be used in the same order every week. The plan is completely yours. Use only the subjects and topics you wish. Remember when planning, that within a class week, the curriculum builds on itself. Whatever you study on Monday will be recognized by your student when you read the story again on Tuesday. When you read the story a third time on Wednesday, the lessons you introduced on Monday and Tuesday will not escape the student's notice as he hears or sees the examples again. So each lesson, except the one for Friday, gets at least one review and some lessons get four reviews. The topics you think are most important, therefore, should be scheduled toward the beginning of the week. It seems as though Art often gets tagged in the Friday slot. Try using this topic earlier in the week, perhaps on Wednesday, so your student can study the pictures for several days as he hears the story read and reread.

Also in the Appendix, you will find a sheet of story disks. These are quick, symbolic representations of the nineteen titles included in *Five in a Row*. They may be used to make a Literary Map. First, color the disk and put the name of the book on the back of the disk. For greater durability, laminate the disks before you cut them apart. Now take a large map of the world (a laminated map is more durable). By placing a Velcro® dot on the disk and the other dot on the map where it goes, you can quickly take it off and put it back on each day. Teacher's tacky putty will also work, and you or the student can locate the disk and attach it daily. Eventually you will be able to track the stories you have read all

over the world. Even young students will learn some map basics. Any stories with ficti
tious settings can be placed in the margins of the map as the "Land of Make Believe."

There is also a blank page of disks in the Appendix so you can make your own pictures for these stories, or replace a lost disk. You might also like to make disks for other
stories you read outside of *Five in a Row*.

Social Studies

Because there are only five subject categories (to correspond to the five days of the
week), many different topics are included under Social Studies. Each story presented has
been identified according to the geographic area. Often the culture of that area is discussed. Making a flag is recommended as an interesting and informative activity.
Geography also includes the mention of oceans, continents and geographic regions. (An
excellent illustrated children's geography book is Rand McNally's *Picture Atlas of the
World*, illustrated by Brian Delf. You'll find it informative and fun!) Under the topic Social
Studies, you will also find lessons about cities, small town life, the homeless, adoption,
occupations, and running a small business. In addition, the Social Studies unit includes
History. Under this heading, you will see lessons which create opportunities to discuss
slavery, civil rights, the Civil War, Veteran's Day, Memorial Day, Labor Day, patriotism,
various other U.S.wars, and explorers like Marco Polo. Social Studies also includes several
lessons about people and their relationships to one another. In this category, you'll find
subjects such as fathering, self-image, stewardship, friendship, taking responsibility, envy,
jealousy, forgiveness, manners, and generational ties-just to name a few. As you can see, a
wide variety of subjects is included under Social Studies.

Choose the topics you'd like to discuss and either mark them in *Five in a Row* or
write them on the Planning Sheet under whichever day it seems best to cover them. If you
use the Planning Sheets, be sure when presenting the material, *to tie it in to the story.*
Finally, in the Geography section of Social Studies, you'll find the directions for placing
the geography disk for each book you read.

Language Arts

There are many techniques for learning Language Arts using children's literature.
Increasing vocabulary, learning literary devices, learning list-making skills, composing
short stories, and acting out dramas are just a few of the ways. Teaching Language Arts is
a natural extension of the enjoyment of children's literature.

Vocabulary is enriched by hearing new words like regatta (*Papa Piccolo*), moonjellies (*Night of the Moonjellies)* or squinting (*Who Owns the Sun?*). A child's vocabulary is
much greater that just the words he can read or spell, and reading a story which contains
new words five times in a row will help increase his recognition and understanding of
those words.

Two methods for organizing vocabulary words are the file box and the notebook.
The file box method uses four by six inch, unlined index cards with alphabet dividers.
Either the teacher or the student can print the word at the top left of the card. Write in a

short definition at the left and either draw an illustration, or cut a picture from a magazine to show the word visually. Keep the words alphabetized and encourage your student to go through the cards frequently. This will help him remember which story each word was from. (To help in remembering the source, write the name of the book on the back of the card.)

A second method of keeping track of vocabulary words is to list them on a page in the Language or Vocabulary section of a notebook. Print the word (large, if necessary) and illustrate with a drawing or magazine picture as a visual reminder. Each list could be alphabetized. Review these words from time to time while remembering your favorite incidents in the corresponding stories.

A notebook is good for more than just vocabulary words. In fact, it's a great way for a student to keep his work organized and ready for quick review and easy reference. For the grade-level student, this isn't unusual. But for the pre-schooler to have *his own* notebook is special. For him, use colored dividers so he can find the subjects, even if he cannot yet read. In this way, he can proudly find his Science section and show someone his drawings or projects. He'll be able to look up his Vocabulary section with illustrations and share his Art work with others.

List-making is another Language Arts skill that develops vocabulary, memory, associations and creativity. It is also a skill that has lifetime value in many different areas, from grocery lists, lists of people to invite to a party, "to do" lists, lists of ways to solve a problem, to descriptive lists that inform. There have been great eloquent lists made by famous people of the things they liked, disliked, or the things they wished for. Once, while travelling together in a car, a friend's family began an oral list of methods of transportation. Many miles down the road, the list had grown to gigantic proportions with the hilarious inclusions of walking on stilts and walking on your hands added to the regular methods of riding in a car, bus, taxi, etc. What began as a list-making exercise became entertainment. The art or skill of good list-making is included in this curriculum to provide both a learning experience and a *good time*.

There are many literary devices explained in this book and tied in to the lessons from children's literature. You probably will not cover them all, but they are included to remind the teacher of them and give opportunities for casual inclusion in the reading lessons.

As you come to each new literary device, a list can be made with examples and pictures. Keep your list in the Language section of the student's notebook. For instance, personification (giving human qualities to non-human things) might be defined and illustrated with a magazine picture of the Pillsbury Doughboy® which depicts a lump of dough made into a person. There are many examples of Personification in such pictures. The other devices can be illustrated, as well. Keeping a chart or list of these words makes review easy and interesting and can be used by the student as an inspirational list when he is creating his own works.

Ideas for leading your student into writing include letting them tape record their stories, which you then transcribe. Often the student will enjoy listening to his own story tape. Writing rebus stories, where a picture takes the place of a certain word throughout the story, is an interesting way to begin writing skills. As you follow the curriculum, you'll find lessons in what makes a good story, and ways to achieve variety. Your student will begin to appreciate the choices an author makes to create a story and the careful thought that goes into writing.

Many times in this curriculum these type of questions are asked: "How does the author make the story exciting? What words does he use? How does he ...?" Eventually, as he sees these techniques modeled before him, the student will begin to include such elements in his own writing. The suggestion after every lesson to imitate an aspect of the author's work is optional, depending on the interest and abilities of the student. See if your student enjoys imitating the author's techniques. If not, just concentrate on appreciating the lesson. In time the rest will follow.

If, however, your student enjoys writing "after the manner of," imitating aspects of the author's story, he will like the suggestions to try a fable, an instructional story or a poem. He'll also begin to include a good setting, interesting characters, an exciting climax, or an important denouement (final outcome of story) in his own stories. Each of these is a separate lesson in the curriculum. Again, keeping a chart or a good notebook list filled with definitions and examples will give your student ready reference when he is writing his own stories and makes review easy. Just add to the list or chart on an on-going basis as you come to different lessons. You might title the chart or list: *Choices A Writer Can Make.*

Remember, there are too many language topics to be covered in a single day. Choose the ones appropriate for your student and jot them briefly on the planning sheet under the day you think best. Remember, if you are going to teach vocabulary it is a good idea to do this at the beginning of the week, perhaps on Tuesday. As the book is read and re-read throughout the week, your student will see familiar vocabulary words again and again, providing a built-in review. Choose only a *few* words from each story.

Art

When you choose good children's literature, you will frequently discover exceptional illustrations, as well. Watercolor, pastels, charcoal, beautiful colors, active lines, funny characters, and balanced compositions are all parts of fine illustrations for children. Furthermore, they can be used to introduce even young children to fundamentals and techniques of art.

Appreciating art is learning to recognize the many techniques and concepts which combine to produce effective art while learning what you like and why. Some pictures have a rhythm, balance and choice of color that combine to make them pleasing. Some illustrations are meant to evoke strong emotions or to provide information. Even young children can begin to identify great art wherever it's encountered. They'll also begin to know *why* they like it. By teaching about the artist and their methods, your student's taste in art will expand to include a rich and wonderful variety of work.

As you look at illustrations with your student, ask "What do you think the illustrator used for his medium?" Sometimes it's hard to tell. There are combinations of pen and ink with water color washes, etchings with strokes from oil or acrylic, and the wet, transparent blends of watercolors. Look for the shading in a charcoal or pencil sketch, or the build up of color by successive layers of colored pencils. Learn to identify the deep texture of pastels.

After you've discussed the medium, ask "why and how" questions. "Why do you think the illustrator chose this medium, color, style, view point, etc.? How did the artist make it look like night time, etc.?" These kinds of questions will open a doorway to art appreciation for your student.

Let him study the illustrations as he tries to answer your questions. You may want to suggest some answers as you discuss the methods the artist used and how the illustrations help tell the book's story. Does the artist's work provide additional story information not included in the text? Does the choice of color palette convey the tone of the story?

Asking lots of questions will cause your student to look with a more critical eye. He will pore over the pages to find answers and he will gain a love of art based on newly-discovered information. This will lead to an emerging appreciation for great illustrations. Don't ask all the questions at the same time. Bring them up conversationally from time to time as you study each book.

One of the best techniques for teaching art fundamentals is to imitate a particular technique from the painting or drawing of a known artist. In *Five in a Row*, the lessons attempt to identify and single out a specific artistic element and to encourage imitation. Your student will be invited to mimic specific styles, colors, designs, etc. Remember that appreciation usually precedes imitation. Therefore, look for examples of the element you are studying in other books, magazines, etc. Let him examine and enjoy these additional examples before he begins experimenting with the technique himself.

In order for you to be ready to meet your student's needs, you may want to have certain supplies on hand:

Kneadable eraser
Drawing pencil or #2 lead pencil

Charcoal	(**Teacher's Note**: Supervise the use of charcoal, since it can get messy!)
Oil pastels	The favorite medium of many young students. They don't smear as much as chalky pastels. (**Adult supervision required.**)
Markers	
Colored pencils	Look for good colored pencils. They make a difference.
Crayons	
Water colors	Prang® brand is good, or tube water colors are extremely easy to use for mixing exercises.
Acrylics	Not necessary, but it gives your student a chance to paint layer upon layer using lighter colors on top.
Brushes	You'll need brushes with several different bristle lengths and widths. If you want to paint fine-lined tree branches, you'll need the right brush!

Water color paper
Canvas paper for acrylics
Drawing tablet or paper
Tracing paper
Ruler
Templates of various geometric shapes cut from cardboard.

Above all, remember that creative art is an intensely personal subject. If you wish to demonstrate a technique, do it on a separate piece of paper-never on your student's own work! Be wise with your criticism of his progress. Grant him the respect you would grant any artist. Go slowly, letting him *catch* the enthusiasm for the ideas you present.

Math

In many of the books chosen for this curriculum, young children ages four through eight will enjoy finding practical ways to use the new concepts they learn in math.

For the youngest student, there are many opportunities for counting practice. It may be counting the stars in one illustration or fence pickets in another. Finding and counting all the cats in *Papa Piccolo* can be fun. It will also provide a time for the teacher to see and hear his student count actual objects.

Ordinal numbers are covered in the material of *Very Last First Time* and you will find an introduction to Roman Numerals in *The Glorious Flight*.

The concept of relative size, measuring, time, and money are all found in the stories of children's picture books. A book about quilts offers a chance to talk about geometric shapes. Because the concepts are linked to an enjoyable story, your student will remember them with pleasure.

If time is available, especially in the summer before school starts, make math manipulatives using ideas from the story illustrations. For instance, if you are going to read a book for a week that is about trains, make flash cards with the facts printed inside train cars. Use bright cheerful colors and write the answers on the back. Laminating the cards will help them last. The cards can also contain any term or new concept on one side with the definition on the other.

(front)

(back)

(front)

(back)

Reading the lesson story all the way through while enjoying the closeness of the teacher and the entertainment of the book establishes a good environment for presenting a math lesson derived from the story. Even the lesson will be a shared experience. If there are more math ideas than are appropriate for one day, choose the ones you wish to cover and write them on the planning sheet for the day you wish to cover Math.

Science

Open wide the door to children's literature and find within the stories a vast array of scientific educational potential; from gazing at the stars and wondering about our sun, to discovering shadows and reflections, insect growth, how a lever works, volcanoes, pollution, seasons, nutrition, animal behavior and much more.

After reading the book for the day, bring up conversationally the science topics suggested in the lessons and other ideas that you may have. Don't try to use all the topics. *Who Owns The Sun?* for instance, includes topics of seasons, five senses, simple machines, weather (rain and wind), stars and our sun. Just choose the ones you think are appropriate and mark them on the planning sheet on whichever day seems best.

When presenting your science lesson, *be sure to tie it into the place in the story.* For instance, in *Night of the Moonjellies*, you might say, turning to the first page, "Remember when the boy was at the beach? What kind of things might you find at the beach?"

A science section in your student's notebook with a page for Ocean Life, a page for Simple Machines, etc., will help in reviewing lessons he's studied. If he likes, let your student illustrate the topics with his own drawings of the story. This could be part of a beloved notebook by year's end.

Note: Throughout *Five in a Row* you'll find students referred to as "he". Obviously, this is strictly a literary convention to avoid cluttering the book with hundreds of, "he and or she" clauses! *Five in a Row* was created to be gender-neutral and you'll find hundreds of fascinating lessons to appeal to both boys and girls. And, please note that we've referred to "teacher and student" in the singular. Many of you will have more than one student. Another item of note is that throughout the lessons, some words have been defined within parentheses. This is done to remind teachers of very young students that even *seemingly common* terms may have to be explained! **Also, see ideas for Review Week p. 120.**

THE STORY ABOUT PING

Title: The Story About Ping
Author: Marjorie Flack
Illustrator: Kurt Wiese
Copyright: 1933
Category: Classic
Summary: A duck learns there are worse things than taking the consequences for one's mistakes.

Social Studies: Relationships - Discernment

Ping learns on pp.16-18 that everything that looks good (like the rice cake trap) isn't necessarily good. Discernment is an important life skill that comes with maturity. You can discuss with your student examples of things which may look better than they really are. Discussions might include offers of candy from strangers, smoking cigarettes, or diving into unfamiliar ponds or streams.

Ping runs away because he doesn't want to take his punishment. He discovers that the loneliness, fear and danger he encounters are far worse than any punishment he might receive. In the end, Ping learns that family relationships and a sense of community are a vital part of life. Everyone is tempted to avoid the consequences of his mistakes. Consider sharing an example from your own life of trying to run away from consequences or punishment.

Social Studies: Geography - China

The Story About Ping takes place along the banks of China's Yangtze river. (YANG-see) Longer than any other river in the world except the Nile and the Amazon, the Yangtze is nearly four thousand miles long. Discuss with your student how long four thousand miles is by comparing it with a familiar distance. You might say, "Grandpa's house is four hundred miles away and so the Yangtze is like driving to grandfather's house ten times." You can also compare it with how far your student went on vacation last summer, etc.

The Yangtze is so wide in places that you can stand on one bank and not see the other shore. Ask if the student has ever been to one of the Great Lakes or to the ocean.

From these places you can't see the other side either. Imagine together what it might be like to live on such a long and, in some places wide, river.

Nearly one third of China's population, 350 million people live on or near the Yangtze river. In fact one of every fifteen people in the world live along the Yangtze. That's half again as many people as live in all of the United States combined. Help your student visualize how alone and frightened little Ping must have felt on such a huge, busy river. Be sure to place your geography story disk where Ping lived—in China, and on the Yangtze River!

Social Studies: Geography - Culture

As you read about Ping, point out the traditional clothes, hats, hair styles, houses and boats (one type of boat is called a "junk") of Chinese culture. Wonder with your child about life on a boat! Discuss the differences and similarities between our culture and the Chinese. In America, for instance, there is a long history of people living on house boats sometimes called "shantyboats" along the Mississippi River and throughout the bayou country (a small stream that wanders through lowlands or marshes) of southern Louisiana.

You may also want to discuss the eating of duck as a delicacy in traditional Chinese cooking. Little Ping nearly becomes someone's special dinner when he leaves the safety of family and friends. Ask if your student has ever eaten at a Chinese restaurant. What sort of foods did people eat there? Did they use chopsticks? Has the student ever eaten duck? Do you think people along the Yangtze ever eat pizza or hamburgers? Have a rice lunch!If you have an older student listening in, he could research the foods of China and help pre-pare a special Chinese meal, which you might eat sitting on the floor around a low table.

Literature: What is a Classic Story?

This book is a classic. A "classic" is a book that generations of children have enjoyed. Ping was written in 1933. Even though the lifestyle, clothes and boats of the peo-ple in China may not be the same today as when Ping was first written (the Chinese do sometimes eat hamburgers!), the story of Ping is still as fresh today as it was in 1933.

When you begin any new book with a student, help him calculate how many years have elapsed since the story was written. You might try to identify an individual whose life dates from the early 1930s, in order to help your student comprehend how many years Ping has been in print. For example, you might say, "When Ping was written, your grand-mother was about your age." Because Marjorie Flack wrote this story about Ping that you, your parents and grandparents could all enjoy when you were children, someday, perhaps your student's children and grandchildren will enjoy Ping, too. That's what makes Ping a "classic."

Literature: Fiction

Explain that fictional stories originate in the author's imagination and therefore are not necessarily true. Explain that often a fictional story begins, "Once upon a time...."

You'll find other stories included in *FIAR* which also begin "Once upon a time..." and you'll want to call the student's attention to this fictional device each time. You can even allow your student to make up their own fictional story which begins "Once upon a time...."
Note: There are occasional non-fiction stories that have the "once upon a time.." beginning but they are the exception. This is most usually a fictional story starter.

Literature - Literary Device: Repetition

The story of Ping both begins and ends with a list of Ping's family members. Throughout the book, the author makes repeated references to Ping's family. The use of repetition as a literary device helps bring the reader "full circle" and provides both a continuity and a sense of completion when the book is finished. Younger children particularly love the use of repetition. Many stories are built on repetition and children often memorize the familiar phrases and passages. Your student might enjoy creating his own story using repetition.

Art: Medium

See if your student can recognize what medium Kurt Wiese used in illustrating Ping. Most of the illustrations look like colored pencil or crayon. Encourage the student to try using colored pencils to do an illustration of their own. Notice how Wiese combines colors to create new tones in the sky on p. 9. At first glance, the sky appears gray, but have your student look closer and discover the variety of colors the artist has used to create the appearance of an evening sky. Similarly, notice the many colors Wiese used for the background on p. 32. Try using multiple colored pencils to create various effects.

Art: Drawing Water

Illustrator Kurt Wiese has drawn water throughout *The Story About Ping*. Discuss with your student the use of broken reflections to give the impression of water. For example, on p. 4, Wiese shows the sun's reflection in the Yangtze's surface. Cover up the reflection with your hand and see how the illusion of water is lost. Give your student a chance to try drawing his own sun and reflection to give the impression of water.

You'll also want to note the use of small, irregular blue circles to show puddles on p. 22 beneath the boy. Let your student try drawing a simple figure like the ice cube below and adding "puddles" beneath it. Note the use of ripples on p. 15 to illustrate action. Allow your student to try drawing broken, irregular circles around any object and see how it suddenly appears as if the object is surrounded by water. On pp. 10 and 14 Wiese has used trailing wavy lines to show motion. This pattern is repeated behind boats, ducks, etc., to create the illusion of movement. Let the student add trailing wavy lines to a simple boat drawing and discover how the boat suddenly appears to be moving. If your student can't draw a boat, draw one for him, or use a magazine photograph and let him draw the background motion lines. Or try a line of ducks, each with their own wavy lines behind them!

Art: Viewpoint

The cover illustration shows Ping from a traditional viewpoint. Ping's profile, the outline of his wing, tail and bill all help to identify Ping as a duck. But, discuss with your student Wiese's use of a head-on point of view on the title page. Without the profile, bill, etc., Ping looks quite different.

Notice how the illustrator has drawn Ping from many different points of view such as "bottom up" on p. 6, "head beneath wing" on p. 9, and "swimming away" on p. 12. Have your student try drawing an egg or a football in profile. Now have him draw it again looking end-on. Point out how our **viewpoint** changes the way we see the world around us. Discuss how picking a different viewpoint adds variety and can make everyday subjects more interesting. Encourage your student to try drawing like Kurt Wiese, by exploring common subjects from uncommon points of view. In an excellent story called *Daniel's Duck* by Clyde Robert Bulla, a young artist tries an uncommon viewpoint for his hand-carved wooden duck. (**Note:** You will see *Daniel's Duck* mentioned again as a featured story in *FIAR*, Vol. 3. Now, see if you can find it for a single reading relating to this lesson in viewpoint and compare the illustrations of Weise and Bulla.)

Art: Unity of Theme Through Subject

The illustrator has used the Yangtze river as the recurring theme which creates a sense of unity by tying the entire book together. Count the pages on which the river appears. You'll discover only three illustrations which do *not* include the Yangtze. Kurt Wiese has provided both unity and context through the repetitive theme of the water. We come away with a sense that for those 350 million people who live along the Yangtze's shores, the river is a part of everything they do. As a teacher, watch for the use of recurring themes, built around a particular subject to create unity in other books you may read with your student.

Art: Composition

Every good drawing has good composition. Turn with your student to p. 9. Discuss how Kurt Wiese has created a diagonal from upper left to lower right with the foliage. This diagonal line divides the illustration into two halves. Each half includes a yellow highlight; the sun in the upper right, and Ping in the lower left. Notice how the grass fronds in the upper left create opposite diagonal lines.

Have your older student sketch some balanced compositions. Have him try pictures which are balanced diagonally, horizontally and vertically. Your student can even cut magazine pictures and place them in pleasing balanced compositions if he does not yet enjoy a lot of drawing. Encourage your student to look beyond content and think about composition whenever looking at an illustration. While good content makes an interesting picture, good composition makes for a pleasing picture.

Math: Counting Skills

Have your student count Ping's family including: mother, father, two sisters, three brothers, eleven aunts, seven uncles and forty-two cousins. Don't forget to include Ping! To make the counting more fun, have the student draw a picture illustrating all of Ping's family surrounding Ping. Some students might prefer tracing a duck "template" on yellow construction paper and cutting out Ping's family and gluing them on a hand-painted Yangtze river. For your very young student, you might use blocks, coins or clothes pins to account for each member of Ping's family. Arrange and rearrange the items as you count them together. Some children might enjoy counting *all* of the ducks or all of the boats in the book as well.

Science: Animal Kingdom

In *The Story About Ping* your student will be introduced to the animal kingdom by learning about ducks. What is Ping trying to catch when he misses the call on p. 6? Ducks search beneath the water's surface for insects, plants, small fish and snails. They look funny with their tails up. Many ducks also enjoy eating bread crumbs. Discuss how Ping's love of rice cake crumbs on p. 15 nearly gets him in trouble.

Ask your student if he or she has ever "fed the ducks". Consider going to a nearby lake or park to feed the ducks bread crumbs and watch them dabble (poke about in the water) as they forage for food. The more time you spend observing, the more you'll learn about ducks! For more information about ducks, get *The Little Duck,* by Judy Dunn.

Science: Buoyancy

The illustrations on pp. 16 and 17 show a boy swimming with a barrel attached to his back. Ask your student why the boy is wearing a barrel.

Both the wood and the air inside the barrel help the boy float, much like a life-preserver helps a water skier. The barrel works on the same principle of buoyancy as a fishing bobber, inflatable pool toys, etc., since both air and wood are lighter and less dense than water.

Try finding which things float in a pan of water: a cork, penny, fishing bobber, pencil, tennis ball, golf ball, etc.

Science: Health and Safety

The boy and his barrel can also provide a good opportunity to discuss water safety. Discuss the role of lifeguards, life preservers and the dangers of swimming alone in unfamiliar water, etc. Even the best of swimmers can get caught in currents and life preservers provide an added measure of safety, like wearing seat belts in the family car.

Science: Reflection of Light

See if your student can figure out why you see reflections on water. Look at the illustrations which show reflections. Discuss the fact that shiny surfaces "bounce" light, reflecting it in new directions. Take a small mirror and do some simple experiments. Try reflecting sunlight onto the ceiling or opposite wall. Now take the mirror and lay it flat on a table. Place various objects on the mirror and look at their "reflections" off the shiny glass surface. If you live near a pond or lake, go there and look at how the shiny surface acts as a mirror, reflecting the image of shoreline trees, boats, the sun, etc.

A.A. Milne wrote a poem entitled, "The Mirror". It can be found in the book of poems called *When We Were Very Young,* or in the combined volume called *The World of Christopher Robin.* One line says,

> "And there I saw a white swan make
> another white swan in the lake."

Milne's poem paints a verbal picture (imagery) of the reflection off the water's surface. Obviously, the second swan was simply the reflection of the first swan on the lake's glassy surface. Perhaps you'd like to find *The World of Christopher Robin** and read it while looking at the lovely illustration which accompanies it.

* **Teacher's Note** to avoid confusion: A. A. Milne wrote two volumes of stories about Winnie-the-Pooh titled, *Winnie-The -Pooh,* and *The House at Pooh Corner.* These story books can be found in bookstores and at libraries under these titles. Dutton Publishers have presented a book with both of these volumes combined. This double volume is titled, *The World of Pooh.*

A. A. Milne has also written two volumes of poetry, titled, *When We Were Very Young*, and *Now We Are Six.* These two volumes can be found in bookstores and at libraries with these titles. Again, Dutton Publishers have also combined the poetry volumes into a single book and called it *The World of Christopher Robin.* Regardless of the format, these books are treasures to be shared and enjoyed over and over! The stories and the poetry have been loved for several generations. They have brought to their readers many moments of shared intimacy, humor, and poignancy. If you haven't had the pleasure of the literary world of Christopher Robin and his friends, explore some of it today!

(**Teacher'sNote**: Re: Lesson Drawing Water, p. 14. *The World of Art - Water - Through the Eyes of Artists* by Wendy and Jack Richardson is a book which showcases twenty artists and their treatment of water. It is copyrighted 1991 by Children's Press, Chicago, ISBN 0-516-09286-3. If you can find it in your library, use it by mentioning the names of the artists and just looking at their interpretations of water. You may find the information about the artists interesting for yourself, but your children will enjoy just looking at the pictures. Drawing or painting water is a fascinating subject!)

Title:	Lentil
Author:	Robert McCloskey
Illustrator:	Robert McCloskey
Copyright:	1940
Category:	Classic
Summary:	A boy discovers that he has a special talent and using it makes a difference.

Social Studies: Geography

The story of Lentil is set in the fictional small town of Alto, Ohio. Use a simple map or jigsaw puzzle of the United States and help your student locate Ohio. Have him find his own state. If your student has done some work with directions, have him determine which direction he would have to travel from his home to get to Ohio. Look at the word Ohio. It begins and ends with the letter "O" and has a "hi" in the middle. Your older student can use that association to help remember the spelling. "A friendly state with an 'O' on each end." Be sure to place your geography disk on Ohio. (If your student happens to live in Ohio, find directions between Ohio and some other state of interest.)

Social Studies: Human Relationships

This story deals with Lentil's self-image and feelings. Lentil can't sing—he can't even pucker, so whistling is out of the question. Ask your student if he has ever been part of a group where the others were all doing something he was unable to do. Ask him how he felt and what he did. *Lentil* provides a great opportunity to discuss individual differences. Discuss the importance of discovering our own uniqueness. Many people go through life feeling inadequate or left out without ever discovering their own gift.

Lentil wanted to make music and he wasn't satisfied until he discovered that he could play the harmonica. In the end, it was Lentil's unique ability which proved to be so valuable. Human relationships are enriched by variety and uniqueness. In order to illustrate the importance of variety, you can have fun discussing what food your student would choose if he could only eat one food three times daily for his entire life. Even if he selects pizza or hamburger, he would probably admit that after a month or two *variety* would begin to sound good. McCloskey's story can help students develop proper feelings about themselves and their own uniqueness.

Hopefully, your student will develop an appreciation for the variety found in his friends and neighbors. Ideally, when we encounter someone who can't do something, rather than ridiculing them, we should find ourselves asking, "What *can* they do?"

Social Studies: Human Relationships - Disagreeable People

Alto's plans are nearly ruined by Old Sneep. Ask your student why Old Sneep is so grumpy and disagreeable. Why is Sneep angry about the town's plans? Discuss how jealousy can make us miserable, unhappy people. Ask your student if he has ever been jealous of someone else's accomplishments? Ask if he has ever known anyone like Sneep. Why doesn't Sneep's plan affect Lentil? (Because he can't pucker, Lentil's problem has become his advantage.) When Lentil uses his talents, the town celebrates in such a grand way even Old Sneep is included in the events!

Social Studies: Life in a Small Town

Discuss the small town of Alto, Ohio. Contrast Alto with your student's own town. Is it larger or smaller? Have your student use building blocks to lay out the town of Alto on the floor. Alternatively, have them draw the town on a large piece of paper or poster board. Help your student label each of the buildings named in McCloskey's story. Let your student draw each of the streets and alleys. (You may need to define *alley* for him, since many towns today no longer have alleys.) Take a toy train or make one from blocks or cardboard and let the student act out the story of Lentil using clothespin characters.

Initiate a discussion about what life is like in a small town. Interesting topics might include shopping, restaurants, crime, gangs, schools, traffic, etc. Compare and contrast these the differences of life in a small town versus a big city.

Social Studies: History

Lentil walks past the Soldiers and Sailors Monument in Carter Memorial Park. Ask your student why people might build a monument to soldiers and sailors who have fought to protect their country. If you know of similar war monuments, cannons or statues in your own area, take your student on a field trip. You can discuss Veterans Day and Memorial Day and their importance to us as Americans. (Veterans Day, November 11th commemorates the end of World War I and honors all United States veterans while Memorial day, May 30th [celebrated the last Monday in May] commemorates all United States soldiers killed in combat.) If appropriate, you can discuss some of the important wars in American history including the Revolutionary War, Civil War, World Wars I and II, Korea, Vietnam, the Gulf War, etc. Consider driving by an area recruiting office to allow your student to see someone in uniform and pick up a poster or brochure showing contemporary men and women serving today as soldiers and sailors.

Social Studies: Patriotism

Notice the American flags flying all over Alto when the town decorates for Colonel Carter's celebration. Show your student an American flag and discuss its symbolism. Count the stars which represent each of the fifty states. Count the thirteen stripes which represent the original thirteen colonies. Patriotism is knowing the country you live in, its unique cultural characteristics and identity, and knowing the reasons why you can be proud of it. Ask the student if he can think of any reasons he's proud of his citizenship. (Answers might include, 'We're free. We help other countries with food and medicine. We protect other countries, etc.")

Social Studies: History

Lentil was written in 1940. Look through McCloskey's illustrations with your student and discuss how things have changed in more than half a century. Pay particular attention to the old-fashioned automobiles, school desks, cash register, nail barrels, bathroom sink, steam locomotive, passenger trains and horse drawn carts. Ask your student which of those old-fashioned experiences sound like fun even today.

Literature: Elements of a Good Story

Setting the Stage	Lentil begins by introducing the location and characters and building excitement in anticipation of the Colonel's visit.
Conflict	Old Sneep's jealousy of the Colonel's success unfolds.
Rising Action	McCloskey lets the reader learn more about the town's eagerness to greet the Colonel and Old Sneep's plan to disrupt the celebration.
Climax	Sneep sets his plan in motion and everyone holds their breath as Lentil saves the day.
Denouement	(day new MAHN) it is the final revelation and outcome; The Colonel is happy and honored and Sneep has a change of heart.

Help your student write a simple story of his own, incorporating these five basic principles of good storytelling. You can write the story down on paper, act it out as a play or videotape it as a movie if you wish. (**Note:** For your younger student, concentrate on only one element, such as the climax. Try writing a story together emphasizing that particular element of a good story.)

Art: Medium

Ask your student to examine Robert McCloskey's illustrations and see if he can guess what McCloskey used to draw them. Your student may answer "pencil", but in fact McCloskey used charcoal. Draw the student's attention to the subtle shadings the artist used to give his characters a rounded three-dimensional form. Notice the use of shadows. Take a look at the faces. Notice how much personality each individual seems to have. The artist has used exaggerated eyebrows and mouth shape to help bring each character to life. If you have a small piece of drawing charcoal, let your student try this new medium on a piece of paper. If no charcoal is available, use a soft pencil to experiment with shading, shadows and facial expressions.

Art: Every Picture Tells a Story (Detail)

While covering the illustrations with your hand, try reading the page where Lentil attempts to sing and only strange sounds come out. Your student will discover that both the words and the pictures contain part of the story. The detail in McCloskey's illustrations helps convey how strange Lentil's sounds must have been. Point out the dogs and cats running away (this action is not mentioned in the text). Notice Lentil's own expression of surprise and dismay. Good illustrations *help* tell the story, adding more detail than is included in the text. Encourage your student to illustrate a simple story of his own with drawings that help tell the story.

Art: Architecture

Take a close look at Colonel Carter's house. Have your student point out the unique and unusual features of the Colonel's mansion, including the lightning rods, shutters, peculiar roof line, weather vane, round-windowed cupola, decorative trim brackets beneath the eaves and the canopied entryway. The Colonel's house was probably built in the late 1800s in a style known as Second Empire, referring to a French architectural style of the 1800s. The unique roof shape is called a mansard roof, named after the French architect Francois Mansart during the time of Louis XIV. Consider driving through an older area of your own town and looking for Second Empire homes or homes with mansard roofs. Look at other unique architectural styles and discuss how design has changed over the years. For your older student, there are several good children's books available on architecture including:

> *Old House, New House* by Gaughenbaugh and Camburn
> *I Know That Building* by D'Alelio
> *Under Every Roof* by Patricia Brown Glenn

If your student has a considerable interest in architecture, check for these or other books at the library and discuss them in more detail. Consider having your student draw a simple floor plan or exterior drawing of a house in which he'd like to live. Your older student may want to draw several elevations (front view, side view, etc.), as well as a floor plan. If you happen to have access to a real set of blueprints, perhaps of your own home, allow your student to examine them, comparing them to the finished structure.

Art: Musical Skill

Ask your student to identify the musical instrument Lentil decided to learn to play. McCloskey says that Lentil "decided to become an expert" at playing the harmonica. Does Lentil become an expert harmonica player over night? Lentil practices "whenever and wherever" he can. Becoming an expert at anything requires commitment, dedication and practice. Try to locate a harmonica for your student and invite him to attempt playing. Ask him how long he thinks it might take to become expert at playing the harmonica.

Mathematics: Introduction to Fractions

Have your child look at the musical notes on the pages wherever Lentil plays his harmonica. If your student plays an instrument ask him if he can identify any of the notes on the page. If not, explain that musical notes come in several "sizes", including whole notes, half notes and quarter notes.

Now, using an apple or banana for a "learning snack", discuss the concept of "whole". Have your student cut the snack in half and talk about how two halves make up one whole. Cut each half in half and introduce the concept of quarters. Two quarters make up a half and four quarters make up a whole. You may want to get out a dollar bill and several quarters as well. Your student can compare a quarter dollar with a quarter apple and a quarter note. Each one is one quarter of a whole and it takes four quarters to make up a whole unit.

Science: Human Anatomy - Taste Buds

Old Sneep's plan for destroying the town's celebration includes the use of a lemon. In sucking on a lemon, Sneep causes all of the band members to "pucker up" so they can't play. Why do sour things make us "pucker up"? Discuss taste buds with your student. The human tongue has approximately five million taste buds which are capable of identifying taste. We replace approximately half of those cells every ten days with new taste buds. We primarily group tastes into four areas; bitter, salty, sweet and sour. Which one of these tastes does a lemon activate? Take a lemon and encourage your student to cut it in half. Each of you take a half to taste or suck on. Discuss the unique sensation of our mouth "puckering up" when we taste something sour. Now that you've sliced a lemon, consider making a glass or pitcher of lemonade. Try mixing two cups of water, three tablespoons of lemon juice and six to eight tablespoons of sugar.

You may want to make the lemonade as a science "experiment" by carefully measuring each component as if you were in a laboratory. For the best flavor, boil the sugar and water for several minutes. Let it cool for a bit and then, add lemon juice and pour it all over ice. As you share a refreshing glass of lemonade together, finish by discussing why watching someone else suck on a lemon can make us "pucker up" as we remember how sour a lemon tastes.

Science: Sound and Acoustics

Find the page where Lentil plays his harmonica in the bathtub. He says "*there the tone was improved one hundred percent.*" Ask your student why that might be. The hard porcelain, tile and vinyl of the bathroom reflect sounds back more clearly, and reverberates without being muffled by carpet, cushions and clothing commonly found elsewhere. That's why you'll often see singers cupping their hand to their ear or wearing headphones in order to be able to hear their own notes more clearly. The singer's hand reflects the sound back to the ear. Suggest your student try singing or playing an instrument in the bathroom and listen for the sound to be "*improved one hundred percent.*"

Title: Madeline
Author: Ludwig Bemelmans
Illustrator: Ludwig Bemelmans
Copyright: 1939
Category: Classic
Award: Caldecott Silver Honor Medal
Summary: A spunky girl has her appendix out and demonstrates individuality
              within a her world of order.

Social Studies: Geography

Madeline is set in Paris, France. Have your student locate France on a world map and place the appropriate *Madeline* story disk on the map. Refer to it each day, as you read the story. As you look at the map, you'll see that Paris is located on the Seine river (pron. sane, or sometimes sen) which flows through the city and eventually empties into the English Channel. Have your student examine the picture of the Seine at the end of the girls' first outing. Ask him why so many cities are located on major rivers. Why was river transportation so important in years past? (Supplies were transported on the river.) Is your student's own city located on a river? If so, consider taking a field trip there to examine the riverfront, boat traffic, etc. Use this time to make the flag of France. You'll find it on the book's cover at the top of the Eiffel tower.

Social Studies: Human Relationships

In *Madeline,* the twelve girls demonstrate important character traits.

"They smiled at the good."	They learn to recognize what is good and appreciate it.
"...and frowned at the bad."	They learn what is evil and to avoid it.
"...and sometimes they were very sad."	They learn what is sad and how to have compassion for others.

To demonstrate compassion, people often take or send flowers, notes, and gifts to those in the hospital or who are sick at home. The visits are appreciated by those who cannot get out themselves and the flowers, notes, and gifts are a cheering reminder that people do care.

Make a list with your student of things people could do for someone who is ill or confined at home. The list might include things such as: bringing them their newspapers, getting groceries, mowing their lawn, putting out their trash, taking them meals, and phoning to check on them. It is never too soon to introduce children to the concept of recognizing the needs of others and knowing some ways to help.

Social Studies: History

Madeline was written in 1933. When you begin any new book with your student, help him calculate how many years have elapsed since the story was written. You might try to identify an individual whose life dates from the early 1930s, in order to help him comprehend how many years *Madeline* has been in print. For example, you might say, "When *Madeline* was written, Mr. Smith across the street was about your age." By noticing the copyright date, your student will discover that some stories, like *Madeline*, were written long ago, and some were published more recently. This knowledge will help him evaluate and appreciate the stories' contents and illustrations.

As you read *Madeline*, ask your student to notice the steam-heat radiator used for heating the hospital room. You may want to discover how your student's own house or apartment is heated. Look for the furnace and determine whether it uses electricity, natural gas or propane. Compare it with the use of a coal-burning steam boiler and radiators. Also, take a closer look at the old-fashioned ambulance and bus in the story. If you live near mass transit, consider a brief field trip to ride a city bus. Many students have never ridden a municipal bus before. See if you can find other old-fashioned things in the story.

Language: Literary Devices

Some of the literary devices the author uses to make *Madeline* more interesting:

Poetry   The story text of *Madeline* is one long poem which utilizes rhyme and rhythm. Practice making up rhyming words with your student.

Repetition   Just before Madeline is hospitalized, we read the line "In the middle of the night, Miss Clavel turned on her light and said, 'something is not right!'" This line is repeated near the end of the story to create added interest. The reader recognizes the repetition and says, "Hey! I've heard that before!"

There is also the repetition of daily discipline "... broke their bread, brushed their teeth and went to bed." You may wish to talk about daily routines and the order they bring to our lives.

Mention these literary devices *after* you've read the story. Try to encourage your student to experiment with poetry and repetition to make his own stories more interesting. Your young student should only try one technique at a time.

Language: Vocabulary

appendix   Madeline has her appendix removed. The appendix is a small, sac-like appendage of the large intestine. Try to locate a child's anatomy book and show your student a picture. Make sure you explain that you look at the picture facing it, therefore your student's own appendix is actually on the *right* side of his body!

solemn   The other eleven girls tiptoed with solemn faces when they visited Madeline in the hospital. They were solemn--without any smile or silliness on their faces. We are often solemn when we're experiencing something new and don't know what to expect.

disaster   Miss Clavel was afraid of a disaster when she awoke. A disaster is any sudden calamity.

Art: Architecture

The buildings shown in the illustrations of *Madeline* are real street scenes of Paris. Facing the last page of the story is a list of Paris scenes. Find a book with photographs of Paris. Together, see if you can match the illustrations to the photographs. Through this process, your student will begin to recognize that the illustrations are not photographic (fooling the eye into believing the drawing *is* a photograph), but rather the artist's *impression* of the streets of Paris. The artist's illustrations are easily identified as the actual scene, even though his art work is not "photographic" in style.

Be on the lookout for pictures in magazines, posters, and books of the more common Paris landmarks, such as the Eiffel Tower. Point them out to your student as you notice them. Maybe he will point out some to you. In this way, the learning process is continually reinforced as a shared experience between you and your student. One benefit of enrichment education is that someday your student will see a billboard or a magazine picture (for example) and exclaim, "That's the Eiffel Tower!" As a teacher, it is your pleasure to introduce him to many things in the world around him.

Art: Appreciating Variety

Bemelmans has illustrated *Madeline* with a wide variety of drawings. Some are large, others are small. Some are monochromatic (one color), while others use a full-color palette. After you have read the story together, discuss with your student this variety, examining each page for size and color. The goal here is to help your student understand and appreciate the variety an illustrator can use in one book. If every illustration had been identical in size and color, the book would have been less interesting. Perhaps your student would like to try illustrating a simple story of his own using a variety of picture sizes and techniques. Bemelmans ends the story with a visual fading away as the print diminishes in size. We don't see this diminishing print ending in every book, so it makes *this* page of text more interesting.

Math: Beginning Grouping and Dividing Skills

Take forty-eight blocks, pennies, clothes pins or marbles. Using the first twelve to represent the girls, see how many groups of girls you would have if Miss Clavel divided the girls up into groups of two to walk down the stairs. Now, using the second twelve items, see how many groups would be required if Miss Clavel makes the girls go to the sink in groups of three. Now, using the last dozen, see how many groups Miss Clavel would have if she has the girls eat in groups of four. Finally, line the "girls" up in two straight lines of six. How many groups are there? (two groups of six)

Math: Relative Size and Degree

Madeline was the smallest of the twelve girls. With your young student, explore the concept of smaller and larger. Go one step further and discuss small, smaller and smallest, or big, bigger and biggest using whatever is handy. Finally, if you have a quantity of some household item in several sizes such as fruit, peanuts, etc., have your student sort. Ask him to find the smallest item. Now the largest. Now put all the **large** items in this pile, the **medium** items over here and **small** items in another group.

Math: Symmetry

As you read *Madeline,* you'll discover that many of Bemelmans' illustrations are **symmetrical** (balanced from side to side). Select an illustration with symmetry. An example is the one where the girls are seated at the table. Count the girls: six on each side. Now the plates: six on each side. Find other ways in which the illustration is symmetrical. Have your student arrange common items symmetrically on the table. Now try an asymmetrical arrangement by having your child arrange items in random groups without being balanced from side to side. Many of the illustrations are **asymmetrical** as well. Look at the twelve girls standing in random clusters at the zoo and, again, at the ice skating rink.

Science: Health

On the final pages of *Madeline,* the other girls wish they could have their appendices removed too. Miss Clavel responds, "Thank the Lord you are well!" It's important to protect our health. We can't prevent all illnesses and accidents, but there are many basic good habits we can develop to help preserve our health. Discuss with your student the importance of washing his hands after using the bathroom and before eating. Discuss the body's need for exercise, healthy well-balanced meals, and the importance of rest. You might want to review the pages where the girls practice many of these same good health habits in the story of *Madeline.* Health habits are an area where discipline and order can pay big dividends.

A PAIR OF RED CLOGS

Title: A Pair of Red Clogs
Author: Masako Matsuno
Illustrator: Kazue Mizumura
Copyright: 1960
Summary: Mako receives a new pair of shoes and learns the importance of honesty.

Social Studies: Geography

A Pair of Red Clogs is set in Japan. Have your student locate Japan on a world map globe, or both. Place the story disk on the map. Japan is an island. You may need to define the word **island** for your student.

Social Studies: Japanese Culture

As you read *A Pair of Red Clogs,* your student will discover many strange and different things. He will learn about clogs, post boxes (mail boxes), markets, weather-telling games, and see different hair styles, and architectural styles with strange roof lines. He will also learn about sitting around a low table at mealtime on cushions, and using chopsticks instead of silverware. Your student will see a kimono, which is a loose outer garment with wide sleeves and a sash, traditionally worn by both men and women in Japan. He may also notice the unusual Japanese writing on the shop windows and signs.

You may want to try several Japanese cultural activities. You might eat lunch sitting on cushions at a coffee table. Try using chopsticks and make your own kimono from a robe or gown and sash. These types of cultural activities enrich early learning and make books come alive!

Social Studies: Human Relationships

In *A Pair of Red Clogs*, Mako wants so much to have her clogs like new again that she decides to trick her mother into buying her a new pair. Most people would actually call this "trick" deception or lying.

What saves Mako is her family's tradition of always trying to clean an object before they buy a new one. It was, as Mako said, "what they always did." (This is an example of stewardship-taking care of what you own.) The tradition of good stewardship shown by Mako's parents, and the quiet, gentle wisdom of her mother and father, helps Mako return to the solid ground of honesty. This also gives Mako a desire never to try to trick her mother again.

Ask your student why Mako wants to trick her mother and why the trick does not work. Explore the honesty and trust we need to have with one another.

Teacher's Note: For teachers that love to learn themselves, John Cross Giblin's *From Hand to Mouth: or How We Invented Knives, Forks, Spoons, and Chopsticks & The Table Manners to Go With Them* is a book that will satisfy your curiosity and love of learning.

Language: Storytelling-Reminiscing (Flashback)

The book begins with Mako, as a grandmother, preparing to send a new pair of clogs to her granddaughter. In the process of telling the story, Mako begins to recall a time many years ago when she was a little girl herself. This is a common storytelling technique called reminiscing or flashback, which you and your student can discuss. Be on the lookout for other stories that begin and then lapse into some reminiscing. Let your older student try to write a story using this technique. Encourage him to begin the story with a present time setting and then switch to a time of reminiscing. While he may not be able to remember "*many* years ago when he was young," he can certainly tell a story that has a flashback to "last summer, when on vacation...." Or try telling your student an autobiographical story (a story about yourself) using the technique of **reminiscing** (remembering) about a time long ago. He may enjoy illustrating your story as a project. Hopefully, your student will begin to ask himself whether a story is present tense, past tense or in the future, as he reads. Most stories can be told many different ways.

Language: Vocabulary

lacquer	Lacquer is a highly polished finish for wood. The lacquer on Mako's red wooden clogs made them very shiny.
suspecting	To be suspecting is to be distrustful or think that someone has done something wrong. Mako's mother did not *suspect* that Mako was trying to trick her.
perfectly	completely, thoroughly and without any mistakes; The mud came out of Mako's red clogs *perfectly*. ·

Art: Colored Pencil Techniques

A Pair of Red Clogs is illustrated with a combination of pencil, pen and ink, and colored pencil. Look closely at the colored pencil portion of the illustrations. Note how Kazue Mizumura has used "cross-hatching" (coloring in more than one direction) to achieve texture. You'll also find that Mizumura uses more than one color of pencil to achieve new colors and shading. Have your student look closely at the illustration of the sunset. Notice how the yellows, reds and blues combine to give shading and new sunset colors. Let him try these techniques in a very simple drawing.

Art: Unity of Theme Through Color

Have your student find which pages do *not* have yellow in them. You'll discover that the artist has used yellow as a unifying theme on every page of the story. Only in Mako's introduction, (before the story actually begins) when she herself is a grandmother, is there no yellow. The repetitive use of one color to give a series of illustrations unity is a good technique. If he is interested, have your student draw a series of three or more illustrations using one predominately recurring color to achieve unity throughout the series of pictures.

Notice that when Mako sits before the fire warming herself, the artist combines red pencil with the recurring yellow to produce a warm, orange color. This gives the effect of heat and warmth. Explain that if your student wants to make something look warm, he can use the *warm palette colors:* yellows, oranges and reds.

Art: Action and Expression in Figures

Explore the illustrations in *A Pair of Red Clogs,* paying particular attention to the action portrayed in the character's bodies. For instance, you can tell, even without seeing Mako's face, that she is full of wonder at the things she sees in the market window. The tilt of her head portrays the emotion. In addition, look at how the artist shows Mako's pride as she wears her new clogs. Her chin is lifted, arms held out and she has a prancing step. Contrast this colorful picture to the grayed illustration of Mako walking dejectedly home under the street light. Again, we see Mako from the back. Her head hanging down, shoulders drooping. Talk about how the artist uses the bright colors to show happiness and the grayed, dull picture to show sorrow. Have your student try drawing pictures of joyful subjects in appropriate colors and of more solemn subjects in the duller colors. Choices of color and body language are other ways an artists uses to express himself. If drawing is too difficult for the student, try to find other pictures in books, magazines or even at a gallery which match the subject with their choice of colors.

Locate the stick figure tracings in the Appendix. They represent the skeletal **armature** (simplest stick form) of several of Mizumura's illustrations. By matching the sketches to various drawings in the book, try to identify where each tracing came from. Now try making your own tracings of skeletal armatures. Your student will discover that even simple stick figures can express a wide range of activity and motion. Now "flesh out" your tracings with form and color. Let your student work at his own skill level, whether he is just beginning to appreciate Mizumura's action figures, or wants to try drawing some himself.

Math: Counting

A Pair of Red Clogs offers many different subjects for counting. You may want your student to count (as high as he can go) all the clogs pictured in the story. You may choose to count the children in the story or the items at the market.

Math: Playing Store

With your student play market, like the lady in the story who sold the clogs. Use buttons for money and find interesting items to include in your "market". For your older student, make a long list of what should be in the market. Add prices to the items and pretend to play store. Choose several items from the list, have your student add the prices. Pay each other with actual money and make change.

Science: Weather and Weather Forecasting

What is weather? What do we mean by weather? One definition is: the general condition of the atmosphere with regard to temperature, cloudiness, and moisture. In other words, what is the temperature? Are there clouds? Is there any rain, hail, sleet, snow, fog, dew, etc.? Is there any wind?

What is good weather? What do we mean when we say "good weather"? If we have an outing planned at the lake, beach or pool, we mean sunny and warm. If we want to go skiing, we mean fresh snow and lots of it. If we're farmers in the midst of a drought, we think of rainy days as "good" weather. What kind of weather does the student like? Which is his favorite season? Discuss the four seasons and the changing weather he can expect in each.

How do we predict weather? How do weather forecasters predict (tell before it happens) the weather? Mako and her friends played a weather telling game, but it was only a game and nothing more. Meteorologists (scientists who study the weather) can and do predict the weather. They use many tools and techniques from thermometers (measuring devices which indicate the temperature) and barometers (measuring devices which measure atmospheric pressure) to photographs taken by satellites orbiting above the earth. Watch the weather forecast with your student and make notes about the meteorologist's predictions. Then, see if his predictions are accurate. You can even keep a daily chart for several weeks, recording the high and low temperature, precipitation (rain or snow, etc.)

THE RAG COAT

Title: The Rag Coat
Author: Lauren Mills
Illustrator: Lauren Mills
Copyright: 1991
Summary: Minna needs a coat for school, and finds acceptance through forgive-
              ness and wisdom.

Social Studies: Geography

The Rag Coat is set in the eastern United States. See if your student can point to the *eastern* portion of the United States on a map. Discuss the four basic points of the compass and how we find each direction on a map. You may want to help your student orient his house or classroom in relation to the four compass points, as well. If you have access to a compass, talk about its use as a tool in orienting yourself.

Specifically, *The Rag Coat* is set in the Appalachian mountains, a range of highlands running from Pennsylvania to Alabama. Locate the Appalachian mountains on the map. See if you can locate other mountain ranges in the United States such as the Rocky Mountains and the Cascades in the Northwest.

Place your story disk on the Appalachian region.

Social Studies: Appalachian Culture

The Appalachian region has its own unique culture. As you read *The Rag Coat*, you'll see many items of interest. Notice the log cabin on the dedication page. Point out the wagon, dulcimer (a mountain music instrument), the process of carding cotton, Minna's father's overalls, quilting, pot-bellied stove, one-room schoolhouse, clothes, boots, bare feet, butter churn, popcorn popper by the fireplace and the oil lamps and candlesticks. See how many other unusual items you can find.

If you'd like to learn more about Appalachian life, go to your local library and check out one or more of the *Foxfire* books. (ed. by Eliot Wigginton) Your student might enjoy watching the video *Christy,* which is set in the Appalachian mountains in the 1930s and is based on the Catherine Marshall novel *Christy.*

Social Studies: Human Relationships

There are many relationships portrayed in "The Rag Coat." Discuss the warm and loving relationship between Minna and her father. It seems filled with Minna's good humor and her father's wisdom.

Explore the attitude of the quilting mothers who give, even when they themselves have need. Unselfish and kind, they help Minna get a coat and keep her secret. Help your student think of times when he may have given generously, even sacrificially.

Minna dreamed of having good friends when she went to school. Instead, she found that the children taunted her and made fun of her. Obviously this was devastating to Minna. Ask your student if this has ever happened to him, not necessarily at school but anywhere. Ask him how he felt and empathize with the feelings. These are emotions that *everyone* has felt at one time or another.

Ask your student what he did about the teasing and then examine the decision that Minna bravely made. Minna, using the wisdom of her father, forgave her schoolmates and brought about a surprise reconciliation. This is a story that beautifully portrays the *power* of forgiveness.

The last important lesson of *The Rag Coat* is the truth that people do need people. When Minna was hurt by the things her schoolmates said, she went off by herself. When she remembered what her father had told her she made a decision to *return* to the classroom. This meant she had to forgive her classmates because she valued being *with people* and wasn't content to stay on the outside (isolated). There may be a place to share with your student a similar experience of your own or to talk about valuing other people.

Social Studies: Funerals and Mourning

This may be a good time to discuss funerals with your student. Ask if he has ever attended a funeral. How did he feel? Minna's father died and Minna was frightened by all the people who came to their cabin wearing black. She couldn't understand why everyone was wearing black, a color her father had hated. She didn't understand that people wear black to funerals to show respect to the dead. It would have been helpful if someone had explained this to her. If your student has been to a funeral, there may be many things he didn't understand. Like one little boy who was totally confused when a distant relative, attending his grandfather's funeral, commented that the little boy had "his grandfather's nose". He was frightened and confused at the prospect of his grandfather having no nose in the closed casket. Death and funerals can indeed be confusing to small children.

Discuss funeral traditions in your student's family or cultural setting. Perhaps wakes are common, or keening (loud crying). He may have wondered about caskets, embalming or cremation. Go only as far as seems appropriate, but many students *will* have questions.

Minna wanted to remain close to her father, even after his death. She wanted a piece of her father's work jacket sewn into her crazy quilt coat. She also wanted the feed sack he had wrapped her in to be the lining of her coat. Pursue this topic with care and sensitivity as you discuss these important issues with your student. Dying is a natural part of living and even small children need honest answers to difficult questions.

Language: Stories

Minna exclaims, "My coat is full of stories, stories about everybody here." Quilts have traditionally been used in literature to tell stories. If you have access to a quilt and know stories corresponding to the pieces, this would be a good time to have fun and discuss them.

Make a simple pieced pillow top using materials that have meaning for the student. Let him tell or write down the stories, sharing his memories of the fabric pieces.

In addition, there are several good books written around the quilt theme:

The Patchwork Quilt by Valerie Flournoy
    A young girl steadfastly works on the quilt her Grandmother began.

Sweet Clara and the Freedom Quilt by Hopkinson
    A creative girl helps slaves escape by hiding clues in a quilt's design.

Stories from Grandma's Attic by Arleta Richardson
    Quilt pieces provide the inspiration for a grandmother to retell stories from her childhood. This series is to be heard aloud and then read over and over!!

Art: Viewpoint

Nearly every one of Lauren Mills' illustrations is of traditional size and viewpoint. The exception is the illustration of Minna and her brother, cowering on a stool by the pot-bellied stove. The giant adult figures, totally out of perspective, tower in front of them. Mills' unique viewpoint helps emphasize Minna's vulnerability. Suggest that your student try drawing from an unusual viewpoint in order to emphasize an emotion or he could cut out magazine illustrations and glue them into a collage. He might have a picture with huge animals and tiny people to emphasize how dangerous the animals are. Conversely, he might have tiny animals with giant children towering over them to emphasize how vulnerable small animals feel. Have your student think of his own ideas. Learning to find an interesting viewpoint is an important lesson in learning to communicate effectively through art.

Art: Warm Palette

In the illustrations for *The Rag Coat,* Lauren Mills uses a warm, subtle palette to convey the impression of warmth, hominess, and Minna's sensitivity. Minna is a gentle girl with a tender spirit, and Mills' choice of colors (warm pastels: soft blues, greens and warm browns) give the impression of gentleness and softness. Imagine how differently the illustration would make you feel if the artist had used bright oranges, purples and electric yellows to illustrate the book.

Let your student try drawing or painting with a limited palette of only two or three colors. (Additional colors can be mixed from these two or three.) What sort of colors would you use to illustrate a science fiction story about a trip to the moon? What about a story of a little girl who wanted to be a ballerina? How about an adventure story set in the jungle? Each story could use a different group of colors. As artists create, their choice of palette colors helps tell the story.

Art: Facial Expressions

Look through *The Rag Coat* with your student and try to name each of Minna's expressions. You might choose words like: hopeful, pleased, happy, intent, loving, frightened, wondering, grateful, eager, admiring, remembering, encouraging, broken hearted, grieving, determined or quietly triumphant. Or, using the above list, ask your student to find a picture of Minna where she looks "eager", etc.

The arrangement of facial components in a drawing tells us what the person is feeling. What makes a face happy or sad? See if your student can draw an up-turned and down-turned mouth. What about surprise? Try drawing the eyebrows much higher than usual. For a look of wonder, try making the eyes big and round. Let the student experiment with eyes, eyebrows and mouth and try to decide what emotion each face is expressing.

Facial expressions are one of the primary ways we tell what someone else is feeling. Whether in life or in books, expressions are important. For excellent lessons on facial expressions, buy *The Big Yellow Drawing Book* by Dan O'Neill. Available through school supply catalogs.

Art: Quilts

Quilts are made like an Oreo® cookie. They have a top, a bottom and a stuffing in the middle. The bottom is usually a piece of solid fabric while the top is made up of many smaller scraps of material sewn together. In between is a soft, fluffy material called batting. Quilt tops, like Minna's coat, can be randomly assembled. They are called crazy quilts. Other tops are sewn in regular, geometric arrangements called patterns. Most quilt designs have well-known names and have been sewn the same way for many, many generations. You can learn a great deal of history by studying quilts because the patterns are named after famous people and events, etc.. Many quilts are "pieced" (made of various pieces sewn together edge to edge). In *The Rag Coat*, the mothers pieces a quilt together in a pattern called Joseph's Coat of Many Colors. This pattern was named after a story in the Bible from chapter 37 of Genesis. You'll find a pattern for this design in the Appendix.

Let your student try making his own quilt block by using geometric shapes. He may color or paint his pattern, or use cut out shapes from construction paper. If you want to sew a quilt block, use a variety of fabric scraps. You can try copying Joseph's Coat of Many Colors from the book's illustration. You can also use the the pattern found in the Appendix. You can even make a crazy quilt pattern like the one in Minna's coat. If you actually sew quilt blocks (enlarge the pattern), use them to make a pillow top, or a small quilt (using several blocks) to snuggle under while reading with your student.

For younger children, try making a *quilt puzzle*. Cut out quilt pieces from cardboard or posterboard and color them like the illustration in the story. Now, have your student assemble the "quilt pieces" to duplicate the original pattern, like a jigsaw puzzle.

Mathematics: Geometric Shapes

The quilting mothers piece a quilt in a pattern called Joseph's Coat of Many Colors. Look at the illustration and see if your student can identify any of the geometric shapes used in the pattern. He should find triangles and squares of several sizes. If he is interested in geometric patterns, you may wish to introduce tangrams. (Tangrams are plastic geometric shapes that can be assembled to create various patterns. They are available from most educational supply catalogs.) You might also make a geo-board by driving short nails in a circle, like the hours on a clock face around a board. Then allow the student to stretch colorful rubber bands or string from nail to nail, creating geometric shapes.

Science: Coal

In *The Rag Coat,* Minna's father is a coal miner. Ask your student what he thinks it would be like to work every day in a coal mine, hundreds of feet beneath the earth's surface. Imagine the darkness and dust. Many coal miners have suffered from black lung disease, a respiratory illness caused by years of breathing coal dust. Minna's father dies from black lung disease.

Coal comes in two types; bituminous (soft coal) and anthracite (hard coal). Chances are your student's grandparents, or great-grandparents remember heating their home with coal. Watch for coal trains in your area, hauling coal to electric generating plants. You may want to check out a book from the library on coal mining and learn more about this important part of America's industry.

Try taking a small flashlight and taping it to a helmet of some sort. Use a football helmet, bicycle helmet, baseball batting helmet or even a winter hat. Tape it in place using duct tape, electrical tape or several strips of masking tape. Now let your student turn on the flashlight and wear the "miner's hat" into a dark room, basement or garage. The light will shine wherever the student looks, just like a real miner's hat!

Science: Natural Fabrics

Where did the fabric for the rag coat scraps come from? There were probably scraps of cotton, wool or linen, provided by the quilting mothers. Show your student samples of each of these various fabrics and discuss their origins. Cotton comes from the cotton plant. It is grown in warm climates throughout the United States and in other similar climates worldwide. You may want to show your student a picture of the cotton gin and talk about Eli Whitney as you discuss the process of carding cotton, spinning it into thread and weaving it into fabric. Linen comes from the plant fiber flax, and wool comes from sheep.

WHO OWNS THE SUN?

Title: Who Owns the Sun?
Author: Stacy Chbosky
Illustrator: Stacy Chbosky
Copyright: 1988
Awards: Winner of the 1987 "Written & Illustrated by..." Award.
Summary: A young boy learns a hard truth, yet perseveres.

Social Studies: History

Who Owns the Sun? may be your student's first introduction to the concept of slavery and its role in American history. This story can provide a jumping-off point to discuss slavery, the Civil War, the civil rights movement, racism, discrimination or desegregation. As the teacher, you can decide how far to go in covering these topics. As you read the story together, you'll feel the pain of both Big Jim and his son. Empathy and compassion provide a healthy gateway to difficult topics.

If you're interested in exploring a related topic, locate a copy of *The Drinking Gourd* by R. N. Monjo. This interesting children's book explores the underground railroad, a system by which slaves escaped north to Canada and their freedom. Place your story disk somewhere in the southern United States as you introduce the subject of slavery.

Social Studies: Family Relationships

Find the pages in which the son asks the father questions about the world around him. Notice that each time the father says that there are things too wonderful to be owned by anyone. Point out, too, that a measure of the son's admiration for his father is that he believes what his father says. He believes in his father's wisdom.

The son also shows a remarkable devotion to his father on p. 21 where he describes his "labor of love". Running with his father's lunch, because he knows how hungry his father is, demonstrates the depth of the son's love for his father. Talk about the many ways that we show people how much we care about them. Point out specific times that you have seen your student show extra care for someone.

The little boy in *Who Owns the Sun?* hears others praise the accomplishments of his father and he is proud of him. But, the boy also hears Mr. Finley say he owns Big Jim and that is a very hard truth to discover. Ask your student how he thinks he would feel if he learned this difficult fact? What would he want to do about it? Now re-read the Afterword and help your student see that in this case it seems that life went on. It was many years later that changes came to Big Jim and his son. One of the life skills demonstrated in this story is the ability to face difficulty and unfairness without becoming bitter. Sometimes we must be patiently willing to persevere and wait for change. Try talking about any of these concepts that seem applicable.

What sorts of unfair things have happened to your student? What kinds of things are people unable to change for themselves? (Answers might include being in a wheel-chair, suddenly loosing a job, etc.)

The son finds out that there are things that his father, no matter how great he is, cannot control. This is an important concept. Big Jim's son must decide how to relate to his father. To learn to continue loving and admiring is maturity indeed.

Language Arts: List-Making

Make a list of the qualities the author uses to describe Big Jim. You might say, "What was Big Jim like?" List the words on a sheet of paper as you and your student remember them together. You may wish to print words like "big hands" with a picture symbol beside them. Finish the list in one day or add to it each day after reading the book.

You could also try listing (with picture symbols) things too wonderful to be owned: stars, sun, flowers, rain and wind. The pictures may be drawn or taken from magazines. Think of other things too wonderful to be owned and include them in your list. This could turn out to be a long list!

Language Arts: Writing

In *Who Owns the Sun?*, the boy asks questions. In fact, it is his questioning that is the recurring thread of the story. Ask your student to make up his own story that asks repetitive questions. An example could be a story that asks several times, "How big is a _____?" or "Why _____?" or "Who told the geese it's time to fly?" or "Who told the bee where to find honey?" Have him answer the questions. In this way, perhaps you'll discover what it is your student wonders about!

You may write out the question story for your student, if necessary. You may want to include pictures after certain words or in place of some words like a **rebus** story. (A rebus is a story that uses certain picture symbols in place of specific words throughout the entire story. For instance, in a rebus story, every time the word cat would be used, a picture is used instead of the letters c-a-t.)

Language Arts: Vocabulary

There are many ways to help your student build his vocabulary. Explain the simple meaning of a word and then use it whenever it is applicable on a day-to-day basis. This helps the child assimilate the word into his vocabulary. It can be a source of togetherness and fun as you share new words with each other.

You may want to keep a chart or three by five index cards as a running vocabulary list for all the books you read together. Pictures beside the words help recall the word for young students. Go over the cards occasionally, just recalling the basic definition.

Some suggested words from *Who Owns the Sun?* might be:

squint(ed) p. 7   To squint is to look with eyes partly closed. Act it out.

windmill   p. 13   A windmill is a mill powered by the wind blowing upon sails or vanes. Find a picture of a windmill.

wander(er) p. 13   To wander is to travel about without plan or destination. When you and your student are outside you could aimlessly walk about and say, "Look, I'm wandering here and there." Acting out words helps students remember.

continue   p. 15   To continue is to keep going or to go on.

Language Arts: Question Mark

Who Owns the Sun? offers an opportunity to discuss the use of question marks. For your young student, let him try to find question marks in the story after explaining their use in ending "question" sentences.

Language Arts: Poetic Prose

The style of writing that Chbosky uses is extremely poetic. She is able, with her highly descriptive phrases, to paint a specific word picture. This is called **imagery**. There is imagery in the description of the April afternoon when the son says, "...my world, now touched by the rays of the sun, smelled sweet. The light that fell across my face felt warm and clean."

Personification, the giving of human qualities to non-human things, is used on p. 9 where it says the cricket cried itself to sleep.

Simile is the comparison of two dissimilar objects, using the word *like* or *as*. On p. 9 you read, "The black sky wrapped around us *like* a soft muffler." The black sky is being compared to a soft muffler and paints for you a word picture that helps you "feel and see" more exactly what the night is like.

There are many examples of **imagery, personification** and **simile** in the text of *Who Owns the Sun?* You many discuss any of these devices and even try a few in writing exercises, or it may be sufficient to simply say, "This writing is beautiful. I can almost feel the sun or smell the rain. This writing is very close to poetry which often makes the reader see, feel and hear more clearly or intensely."

Language: Elements of Story, Climax and Denouement

Ask your student if his feelings at the end of the story would be the same if the Afterword had not been included. Chbosky has ended the story at the point of **climax** (the highest point of interest or action) and, if left here, our feelings might be sad, rather hopeless or highly agitated. The afterword in *Who Owns the Sun?* serves as the **denouement** (day new MAHN) meaning final outcome or action, to let the reader down gently and leave him encouraged.

Art: The Illustrator

The author of *Who Owns the Sun?* is also the person who illustrated the book. Stacy Chbosky is unusual because she was fourteen years old when she wrote the book and painted the pictures for this story. If your student has interest in writing and drawing or painting, encourage him that *young* authors and artists are producing fine work.

Art: Subject and Symbolism

After reading the story, go back and look at each picture. The paintings of Stacy Chbosky show very simple subjects. In other words, the illustrations are simply rendered without precise details. Find a picture of a painting that is complicated in its detail to show your student the contrast to Stacy's illustrations.

These illustrations are very simple, yet they are also strong. The bright (strong) colors, tall trees, and large rocks all add the feeling of strength to the writing. Remember how the authors writes of the strength of Big Jim and then shows that strength in the objects around him. That's symbolism! Again, the lesson is the integration of words and pictures to make a powerful story. Continue to expose your student to these ideas and someday it may become part of his work, too.

Art: Color

Chbosky has used a variety of color in her paintings for *Who Owns the Sun?* Talk about the names for the colors and introduce one or two new color names: chartreuse, pink, mauve, lavender.

Pick a picture (the ones opposite pp. 13 or 15 are good for this) and encourage the student to paint a picture after the same manner. Have him copy the colors (your student will have to try mixing paints to achieve the right color) and try to copy the types of brush strokes. Remember, when layering watercolor you must be patient and let each color dry before adding the next one. This should be fun. There is no right or wrong to this type of experimenting.

Art: Bright Light and Shadows

Study with your student the use of bright light and shadows in the illustrations. The sun is an obvious source of strong light. Examine each picture that includes the bright sun and notice the shadows of the trees, fence posts, rocks and people. Notice the strong shadows, especially the shadow of Big Jim and that of his son on pages 19 and 21. Choose some building blocks and find a window with strong, direct sunlight. Let your student experiment with turning the blocks and seeing the shadows. Notice that in a row of blocks the shadows are all parallel (lay in the same direction.)

Talk about the direction of the light source and that the shadows of the object appear on the *opposite* side of that source. Your student may begin to point out shadows that he sees in illustrations of other books, in magazine photographs, or that he notices himself on a sunny day.

Remind your student that he might consider the direction of the source of light in his own paintings and drawings. By thinking beforehand about the direction of light, he will know on what side of his subjects to draw his shadows! In any case, just seeing a student begin to add any shadows at all is a sign of a maturing artist.

Art: Symbolism

On p. 7 we read, "It was an April afternoon, and my world...smelled sweet." Notice with your student the beautiful painting and especially the beautiful, tall trees. Now turn to p. 25 and read, "He bent down and put his arms around me, and then he began to cry." Look at the trees on that page. Again the words and the pictures tell the story together. The trees symbolize both the happiness and then the loss that we read about in the story.

Art: Figures

Because the illustrator has used very simple human figures without much detail, what becomes very important is the action or motion portrayed. Look at p. 19 and see the action in Big Jim's arms, back and legs as he works at moving the rock. Now see the action in the arms and legs of his son on p. 21 as he runs with the lunch. Finally, examine the great sorrow shown in the drooped shoulders and lowered head of Big Jim on p. 25. We don't need a great amount of artistic detail to see the emotion of these characters. The body language tells the story. Talk about the freedom an artist has to draw some things in detail and to draw other things with meaningful simplicity. Remind your student that he can make these kinds of choices in his art work. Add: Simplicity or Detail? to your list of Choices An Artist Can Make.

Math: Counting

Have fun counting the stars on p. 9, the pickets on the fence on pp. 7 and 21, the flowers on p. 17 and the tree stumps on p. 25. Have older students divide the stars into groups of three. See how many groups there are, etc.

Science: Seasons

Who Owns the Sun? begins in the spring and continues into summer. You may wish to introduce the seasons, review them, or just list the descriptions of spring and summer included in this text. Add any descriptions of your own to the list. Have your student answer questions like, "To me summer is...," etc.

Science: Simple Machines

There are two simple machines included in this story. Shown on p. 19 is a lever. A **lever** is a bar used to pry, move or lift things. It is used with a fulcrum (the balancing point near the center, like a teeter-totter.)

Talk about the help a lever and fulcrum give in trying to move a heavy rock. If possible, find a large rock and try to move it without a lever and then with one. We use levers at other times to pry the lid off a can of paint, etc. (The screwdriver becomes the lever and the outer paint can edge becomes the fulcrum.) Another simple machine used in this story is a **wedge**. This is the axe head shown on p. 25.

Other simple machines (not mentioned in this story) include the **wheel and axle**, the **pulley**, the **inclined plane** and the **screw** (which is really a spiral inclined plane.) Feel free to explore all six simple machines, if your student shows interest.

Science: Five Senses

This story affords an opportunity to introduce the five senses: sight, smell, touch, taste and hearing. There are many descriptive phrases in *Who Owns the Sun?* to introduce a discussion about each of the five senses and what they do.

Science: Memory and Nutrition

What did the mother pack in the father's lunch? How many items can your student remember? How many can you both remember together? Look on p. 21. How many did you remember correctly?

This could be an opportunity to introduce the system of food classification called the Basic Four:

 The milk group for all milk and milk products

 The bread and cereal group

 The meat group

 The fruit and vegetable group

Try to determine if the lunch packed for Big Jim was a balanced meal. With your student, plan a balanced breakfast, lunch, and dinner. Then, have a balanced snack together!

MIKE MULLIGAN AND
HIS STEAM SHOVEL

Title: Mike Mulligan and His Steam Shovel
Author: Virginia Lee Burton
Illustrator: Virginia Lee Burton
Copyright: 1939
Category: Classic
Summary: Mike Mulligan and his steam shovel triumph in changing times.

Social Studies: History

Mike Mulligan's earth-moving shovel was steam powered. The age of steam has been over now for nearly fifty years. Talk about the important part that steam power played in industrial history. There were steam boats on the rivers, steam-powered ocean liners, steam engine locomotives, tractors, threshing machines, steam-powered fire pumpers, steam-heated radiators in homes and businesses, steam calliopes in the circus, etc. The steam engine was the primary source of mechanical power for a century and a half. Today most of our machinery is powered by either electricity or internal combustion engines using gasoline or diesel fuel. That's why steam shovels like Mike Mulligan's Mary Anne are no longer in demand.

Make a list of old machines that were steam-powered (several are pictured in the book). Now make a list of modern machinery and try to determine how each one is powered. (Almost all are powered by diesel engines today including diesel trucks, earth-moving equipment, locomotives, ships, etc.) Some students may want to learn more about steam engines. You'll be surprised to discover that steam engines date to approximately 60 A.D. You may have an old steam locomotive nearby on display. You might want to plan a field trip to explore its giant firebox, boiler, pistons, rods, etc.

As a simple history lesson just look at the pictures of the milk truck pulled by horses, the wagons for people to ride in, the old cars, and the clothes people are wearing (including the ladies hats). See what other things of days past you can find together. Be sure to place the story disk on the United States, or on the margin, in the Land of Make Believe.

Social Studies: Character - Stewardship

Mike Mulligan has taken excellent care of Mary Anne. Good stewardship is taking care of the things we own and the resources we have to use. You may want to talk about the admirable way Mike cares for his steam shovel. We have many chances daily to be careful with the things around us and and use them wisely. You may also want to use this opportunity to introduce the subjects of **conservation** and **ecology.**

Social Studies: Character - Flexibility

When the basement is finished, Mike Mulligan has to come to grips with the changing world. The steam shovel is no longer in demand. Instead, the work is being done by machines powered by gasoline and diesel fuel. Mike Mulligan is willing to deal with changing times, when it is suggested that Mary Anne become the furnace for the new town hall. Rather than becoming angry or bitter because they can no longer do the same kind of work together, Mike Mulligan demonstrates the wise quality of flexibility, and accepts a different way to use their skills.

Social Studies: Human Relationships

Mike Mulligan says he and Mary Anne work faster and better when people are watching. It is fun to work before a cheering crowd, although we also need to learn diligence when no one is watching. Mike Mulligan was boasting a bit when he claimed Mary Anne could dig as much in a week as a hundred men, especially since he "wasn't quite sure." However, he did back up his boast with an agreement to forego his pay if he failed. Discuss the concept of a boast. Try to think together about times when boasting might occur.

Also, in relating to other people, there are sometimes those who seem to lack integrity. That means they may not always be completely honest and fair. Henry B. Swap had a great desire to save money. Swap was so greedy he tried to take advantage of Mike Mulligan, by asking him to dig the cellar and figuring he would get the digging done for free (notice the line," so he smiled in rather a mean way"). As in other stories, by Virginia Lee Burton, the author seems to deal with characters like Henry Swap by having the main character continue to do what is right. Often the uncharitable character begins to change for the better. The author's decision to include those figures who seem mean or unkind lends a reality of life to her stories and allows children a chance to see how others deal with some of the more difficult relationships in life. This is a good time to discuss good manners, being polite and being respectful, even when others are neither kind nor fair.

Language: Story Writing - Characters

Look at all the different townspeople in *Mike Mulligan.* One way to create interest in stories is to have a variety of characters: big, little, young, old, happy, mean, imaginative, etc. Try to write a story with several types of characters. Ask the student to think of the many kinds of people he has known, read about or seen on television. Have him take a characteristic from one person and add it to something he remembers about another person and make what we call a composite character. For instance, an aunt who loves to wear blue may be combined with a neighbor who likes to play the trumpet and dance, creating a fictional, composite character; a woman that likes to wear blue, play trumpet and dance.

For your story setting, you might use a scene with a lot of people such as a movie or the circus. Try using imaginative names like Virginia Burton's did in *Mike Mulligan*. She made up names like Popperville, Bangerville, Kipperville and Kopperville.

Language: Elements of a Good Story

You may want to point out the elements of a story:

Setting:	This is where the story takes place.
Conflict:	Steam shovels are no longer wanted because they're slow.
Rising action:	Mary Anne digs faster and faster.
Climax:	"Then suddenly it was quiet. Slowly the dirt settled down. The smoke and steam cleared away, and.... There was the cellar all finished!"
2nd Conflict:	How will they get out of the cellar?
2nd Climax:	Mary Anne could be the furnace for the town hall.
Denouement: (day new MAHN)	The final resolution or outcome is that Mike and Mary Anne change occupations and make a new place for themselves.

Each teacher has to know his student and present only the amount of information that is proper for that student. You may want to teach only one story element at a time. As your student progresses, it is the goal of this type of instruction to teach all the elements of a good story. In time, he will enjoy finding these elements in stories he reads and eventually will use some of this information in writing his own stories.

Language: Literature - Personification

Personification is a figure of speech in which a thing, quality, or idea is represented as a person. In *Mike Mulligan,* the steam shovel is named Mary Anne and given the human qualities of perseverance (sticking with a job even when it is hard) and heroism (by saving the day through extraordinary effort). You may wish only to draw your student's attention to the expressions on Mary Anne's face throughout the story and to note the way Mike relates to her with affection, etc.

It is fun to name and give personalities to objects. Perhaps the student can already think of times he's heard the family car referred to as "Jenny Sue"or a blanket named "Buddy." Davy Crockett had a rifle named "Old Betsy," and a girl Caroline named her kettle "Maude" which meant "strong in battle." Many people (particularly in Europe) name their houses or estates. Enjoy exploring this topic with your student. Help him think of creative names for his home, neighborhood, family car, etc. Gently encourage your student to include personification in stories he writes or that you create together. Personification can include naming objects as well as giving them certain characteristics of people.

Language: Literary Classics

Mike Mulligan and His Steam Shovel was written in 1939. For more than fifty years, children and adults have enjoyed this suspenseful tale and appreciated the animated illustrations.

Have your older student look up the copyright date on *Mike Mulligan.* Explain to him that the copyright date is usually when the book was first published. Help him find the copyright in several other books which are handy, searching for other "classic" titles. Talk about the definition of copyright. If there is extreme interest help your student find out how an author obtains a copyright for a book.

Language: Vocabulary

canal   a waterway dug across a narrow piece of land; There is a
good picture of a canal in this story. It is also easy to point out the
Panama Canal on a map.

cellar   another word for basement

Art: Drawing - Trees

Turn to the page that begins, "*They left the canals and the railroads....*" Point out the trees on this page. They are the stick and ball type trees, good for aerial views and long distance views but not as good as the trees on the next page for close-ups. Explain how you can draw and paint good branching trees by starting with the bottom of the trunks and drawing upwards, forking (splitting) the branches as you go. Then you can make irregular circles, elongated ovals, etc., for the leaf effect. Your student can practice a time or two and that should be sufficient for an introduction.

Maybe you can point out unusual branched trees on an outing to help make your student aware of variety in trees. Keep a sketch pad and pencil with you to capture quick drawings of an unusual tree, etc. Refer to this sketchbook when it is time for drawing scenes.

Additional practice now and then should help bring the technique to your student's memory and eventually to his work. Art can be an intensely personal subject at any age, so let him student set the pace. It is what he sees, appreciates, and picks up for himself that is important. Remember to demonstrate any art technique on a separate sheet of paper and *not* on your student's own work!

Art: Motion

With your student, look at the picture of Mary Anne in her final climactic dig. See if your student can explain how the artist illustrated the extraordinary effort that Mary Anne was making? Mention the swirling circular motion of the smoke, steam and the dirt that shows the funnel-like powerful movement of the steam shovel. Take colored chalk or crayons and have fun trying to draw an action picture or just making "action" swirls like a design. Use several colors and patterns for different effects.

Math: Application in Construction

Mike Mulligan needs to know arithmetic in order to dig the cellar for the Popperville town hall. He has to dig it "neat and square". Discuss with your student the fact that construction workers and architects (those who design the buildings) need to know a lot of math. If they did not, the buildings might not look good. They might be crooked or possibly dangerous. When you are on outings, point out to your student areas of construction, and remind him that the people working there need to know math!

Math: Geometry

The cellar was completed: "four corners...neat and square." The definition of a square is a polygon with four equal sides and four equal angles (90 degree). Practice finding objects that are square (check by measuring) and draw (either freehand or by measuring) squares on paper. You can also have on hand pre-cut paper squares in various sizes and colors to make a design or a city.

Another project is to use a geo-board made by taking a square board (approx. 12 x 12 in.) and driving nails into it at the same intervals as the hours of a clock. This needs to be measured carefully. You may include a nail in the center. Colored rubber bands or string can be used to create many different geometric designs including squares.

(Squares, for example, can be created by using four rubber bands. Stretch the first from 12 o'clock to 3 o'clock, the next from 3 o'clock to 6 o'clock, etc., or have your student try his own ideas to make a square.)

Math: Counting

Virginia Burton has drawn many interesting things to use in counting practice such as cars, people, telephone poles and houses.

Beyond counting, try grouping. Lay a piece of tracing paper over the scene of the mountain with the pine trees. Ask your student to draw a circle around four trees and continue until all the trees are circled and count the groups.

Or you can say, "if a lumber company wants to cut six trees a day to make way for the train, how many trees could they cut in a week?" In order to figure out the problem, you could use blocks, buttons, pennies or clothespins for the trees. Arrange them in groups of six for each day you count. Then count the total number of objects.

Science: Steam Power

A teakettle of boiling water will move a pinwheel. Find the pattern and instructions for a pin wheel in the Appendix. This shows the simple truth that steam produces power. Depending on the age of your student, you may want to go further with the topic of steam power. You can discuss the use of steam to push a piston in any of the early steam machinery or explore steam turbines. Steam can be used to turn a turbine at high speed for the production of electricity, for instance. Check encyclopedias or your library's card catalog for additional information on steam power.

Science: Creative Thinking-Problem Solving

Everyone in the town argues about how to get Mary Anne *out* of the cellar, but one character looks at the problem in a different way. The little boy wonders what will happen if Mary Anne *stays* in the hole. There are many different ways to solve problems. A good beginning skill for scientific investigation is to be able to wonder "what would happen if," and to look at a problem from many directions. Gently encourage wondering by pointing out that the little boy does a good job of thinking of a *different* way to solve Mary Anne's problem. The next time a problem arises in your day, practice thinking together of different ways to solve it. Remember to look at the problem from as many different directions as possible.

Science: Road Engineering

Mike Mulligan and Mary Anne, "lower the hills and straighten the curves", for roads to be built. In most parts of the country there are road cuts where the rock cliffs rise on both sides of the road. Point them out and talk about the modern machines, drills, trucks and dynamite that make the cuts today. Ask your student why highways are leveled and straightened. (The elimination of hills, valleys and sharp curves make modern highway travel faster, safer and more fuel-efficient.)

THE GLORIOUS FLIGHT

Title: The Glorious Flight
Author: Alice and Martin Provensen
Illustrator: Alice and Martin Provensen
Copyright: 1983
Award: Caldecott Medal
Summary: Papa Bleriot overcomes many obstacles in achieving his goal of flying.

Social Studies: Family Relations

Ask your student, "What can you tell me about Papa Bleriot's (BLAIR-yo) family? What kind of things do they do together?" You may get answers like, "Papa has a wife, three girls, a boy, a cat, dog and a cockatoo. They eat meals together, go driving, kiss each other and watch their father try to fly."

Social Studies: Human Relations-Making Reparations

Papa Bleriot has an accident in his shiny new car. Discuss how, when we hurt someone or damage their things, we need to say we're sorry, try to fix the damage and try to leave the person satisfied and not angry. This is called making amends, or reparations.

Ask your student how Papa handled the situation. If they can't remember, review this story element together. You may recall that Papa was saved by the sound of the flying machine that was a wonder to all. He then invited everyone to the cafe.

Social Studies: Geography

The Glorious Flight begins in Cambrai, France and ends just over the White Cliffs of Dover in England. Papa has successfully flown across the English Channel. This is a wonderful opportunity to introduce your student to the names: English Channel, White Cliffs of Dover, France, and England. Memorization isn't the goal. Just hearing the names is helpful. If you desire, you can place the story disk on France and use a string or narrow ribbon to connect another story disk to England, showing how the flight crossed the channel (a narrow body of water joining two larger bodies of water).

Social Studies: Geography - Culture and History

This story contains many French names: *Louis Bleriot* (BLAIR yo*), Alceste, Charmaine, Suzette, Jeannot* (ZJON-o*), Gabrielle, Minou* (MEE noo), *Arsene, Chloe, Cambrai (*COM bray*)–a city in France, Escopette, Alphonse Juvet* (JOO-vay)*, Cesar, Achille* (a SHEEL) *Duval.*

This true story, based on the life of Louis Bleriot, also gives us a glimpse of life in a small French town between 1901-1909. There are street scenes, shops and the furnishings inside their houses. There are outdoor cafes, vegetable carts, a steam-powered boat on p. l7, and a French flag flying on p. 28. The lady on p. l0 has a baguette (pron. bag - et) in her basket which is a long thin loaf of French bread. The conclusion of the story shows Papa in England and everyone is holding umbrellas. (So you may want to mention England's reputation for rain and fog.)

The auto Papa drives was built nearly one hundred years ago. Notice differences between this car and our modern ones. Answers might include: "Papa's car had no wind-shield. There are lanterns on the front of it instead of headlights. There do not seem to be any rear view mirrors. There is a crank in the front. (Explain how the hand crank started old cars instead of electric starters.) There are running boards and funny fenders and no doors, let alone seat belts!"

Now have a baguette (bag-ETTE) with butter for a treat.

Social Studies: Geography - Flags

It might be a good project to make paper flags of countries that you meet in the stories. They could be displayed hanging sideways on a long string or each with a small stick lined up on a styrofoam block.

Language: Choosing a Title

Point out briefly that the choice of titles for stories, books and pictures is not an afterthought but a carefully thought out part of the work. Notice how the title of this story shows some of the drama and excitement of the triumph of flight. For a good creative exer-cise, see if you and your student can come up with other exciting title ideas for this book.

Language: Italics

The boat on p. 32 will pick up Papa if his motor fails. The name of the boat is *Escopette* and the name appears in a different print from the rest of the story. The name of a boat or ship is written in italics. A student may notice the difference in the print. Mention in passing that the names of ships and boats are written in that different type style. They may begin to recognize italics in other stories. If your student hand writes a story which contains the name of a boat or ship, the name of the ship should be under-lined.

Language: Descriptive Writing

Page 26 of *The Glorious Flight* describes the English Channel:

> "Twenty miles wide.
> Black, tossing waves.
> Fog and rain.
> A very cold bath.
> A long swim.
> It is a dangerous prospect."

You might try using any subject and having your student write or dictate to you descriptive phrases. For instance a student might describe strawberries as:

> "Round and red.
> Thousands of seeds.
> Sweeter than candy.
> Jagged green leaves.
> Funny long runners.
> They are a delicious treat."

This is a prelude to the type of writing skill used in the Haiku poetic form, but there is no need to count syllables. Have fun brainstorming these descriptive phrases with your student.

Language: Poetic Device - Onomatopoeia

The authors of *The Glorious Flight* have written a prose story of Louis Bleriot using the poetic element **onomatopoeia** (owna-mat-uh-pee-uh) words that create the sound of the object as you say them. On p. 12 "listen" to "Clacketa, Clacketa, CLAKETA! CLACKE-TA! This is the sound of the airship. P. 10 also begins with "Crump!", the actual sound of Papa's car bumping into the car of Alphonse Juvet.

Remind your student that using **onomatopoeic** devices in his stories, like writing in sound effects, and adds variety.

Art: Appreciation

The paintings in *The Glorious Flight* are full of color and action, people and sky. The picture on p. 33 shows Papa's face, fully aware of the danger of his situation, and again p. 35 shows that Papa is alone in his adventure.

Art: Perspective and Viewpoint

Pages 12 and 13 are an unusual contrast to the traditional street scene of pp. 8 and 9. Many of the illustrations show people looking up at the sky while others show the viewpoint from the sky downward. If possible, try drawing a picture or two from each viewpoint.

Have fun exaggerating the view. Try to imagine what you'd see if you were high, like an eagle looking down, or very low on the ground like an ant looking up.

For a simple viewpoint project, stand up. Now look down at an apple or toy placed on the floor. Try drawing what you see. Now try sitting on the floor and looking at the same object placed on the edge of a table. Study the difference. Wonder with your student what his home or neighborhood would look like from the air. If he is interested, let him try to draw what he imagines.

Math: Ordinal Numbers

Glorious Flight provides an opportunity to discuss the concept of "first, second, third", etc. Each time Papa tries to perfect his flying machine, you can call it the first try, the second try, etc. You might explore the difference between the numbers 1, 2, 3, and the idea of order, like standing in line and being first or second.

Math: Roman Numerals

Each of Bleriot's machines is named with a Roman Numeral. You might want only to explain that these marks I, II, III, IV are a different way of making numbers. If there is interest, you could continue with the fact that they were used in a country called Rome a long time ago. Show the numerals and their number counterparts to your student. To ten, these Roman Numerals are: I (1), II (2), III (3), IV (4), V (5), VI (6), VII (7), VIII (8), IX (9), X (10).

Science: The Process of Invention

The Glorious Flight portrays a passion for invention. Every passionate inventor understands that you must try again and again until you succeed. Look with your student at how hard Papa tries. He overcomes the disappointment of flights that don't work, crashes with broken ribs, black eyes, breaks, sprains and bruises. He continues to work on his project and finally carries through the dangerous prospect of flying over the ocean. This is the process of invention that scientist and inventors must go through to reach the goals they see before them. Again, notice how the title and the ending of the story lift us up to the thrill of victory "We did it!"

If your student expresses interest, explore other inventors and their inventions. Recognize the same patterns of persistence (sticking to a project), heroism and self-sacrifice. A marvelous book on the invention of rubber is *Oh, What an Awful Mess!–a Story of Charles Goodyear* by Robert M. Quackenbush. You'll find it is easy to read, enjoyable and it certainly reinforces the theme of perseverance.

Science: Flying

Since the beginning, man has admired flying as he watched the birds soar in the sky. Many attempts have been made to copy their flight. If there is interest, get a book from the library on the beginnings of the flight of man. This might be the time to introduce the story of Daedalus and his son Icarus. Icarus, who flew too near the sun, melted off his feathers according to Greek mythology. As your student progresses through school he will encounter allusions to the story of Daedalus in poetry and literature.

If man's attempts at flight especially interest your student, try reading *Ruth Law Thrills a Nation* written by Don Brown, ISBN 0-395-66404-7, or *Lindbergh* by Chris L. Demarest, ISBN 0-517-58718-1, as well as beginning level stories about the Wright brothers and Amelia Earhart.

Be adventuresome and take this opportunity to design and fly paper airplanes!

This is also a wonderful time for a list. Make a list of all the different ways to travel. Include airplanes, hot air balloons, skate boards, snow shoes, buses and many more. If you can find a printer who is willing to supply you, get an end roll of newsprint and make the list a long scroll. You can add to it during the week, as new ideas come along. Your student might also want to include ideas of travel from the future—maybe a future invention!

HOW TO MAKE AN APPLE
PIE AND SEE THE WORLD

Title: How to Make an Apple Pie and See the World
Author: Marjorie Priceman
Illustrator: Marjorie Priceman
Copyright: 1994
Summary: An apple pie is an easy thing to make as long as you have the ingredi-
              ents. If not, hang on!

Social Studies: Geography

How to Make an Apple Pie can be a spring board for many different discussions of
Geography. Choose one country to talk about, or chart the trip on the inside cover map or
on your own map. Be sure to place your story disk on a different country each day as the
story progresses.

This is a wonderful opportunity for your student to begin hearing the names:
Europe, Italy, France, Sri Lanka (sree lanka), England, Jamaica, and Vermont. Hearing
the names of famous places can spur interest when the words reappear at a later time. It
makes it easier to eventually learn them. Years later your student may say, "Oh, I've
heard of Sri Lanka. Cinnamon comes from there!"

There are references to several countries. Ask your student what the artist has
chosen to include in the illustrations that shows what each country is like. Talk about
these choices as you look at each country's pictures.

Italy: You'll find a discussion of the Italian Language (point out that different coun-
              tries speak in different languages.) There is also a reference to the semolina
              (sem a LEE na) a type of wheat used for making pizza crust and
              breads. Notice the white buildings with red roofs.

France: The young baker takes the train to France. Notice the Paris sign on the
              train, and the *l'omlette* sign at the street cafe'. Again, there are buildings to
              see and the Eiffel Tower peeking from in back of the buildings. If your stu-
              dent remembers the Eiffel Tower from the story *Madeline,* he may be
              able to recognize it even though the artist has chosen to show only a portion.
              Note that the bicycle is a common mode of transportation in the rural
              areas.

Sri Lanka: Sri Lanka (sree lanka) is a pear shaped island off the southern tip of India, in the Indian Ocean. As you progress through these lessons, you may wish to introduce the names of the major bodies of water. You can point out the location of the Indian Ocean on the map and make a chart of oceans or bodies of water to be added to at different times. By doing this, the next ocean is added and the first name reviewed. This happens on a continuous basis, as a built-in review. Make an ocean disk from the blank disks to place on the map.

England: Notice the country cottage, vines about the door and flowers in the yard. There are cows on the hill and a castle in the background. There is a reference to good manners and charming accents.

Jamaica: Bananas grow in Jamaica—hence the banana boat. There are palm trees and a sugar cane plantation.

Vermont: Where, in the United States besides Vermont, do they grow apples? (Washington State, Oregon, Michigan, etc.) Research different varieties of apples and let your student hear the different names. Point out the different kinds of apples at a market or orchard. Buy or pick several kinds and bring them home to compare color and taste. Mention that fall is harvest time for apples.

Geography: Memory Game

List where the apple pie baker went. After several readings, let the student try listing the locations in order from memory. If necessary, help jog his memory. She went from _____ to _____ to _____.

Language: Humor in Writing

How has author Marjorie Priceman made her story funny? What are the elements of humor? (Humor is defined as the unexpected; unexpected conclusions, actions, ideas, interpretations and responses.) Ask your student what parts of the story he thinks are funny. How did the author make it funny? Explore the author's use of "traveling all over the world" to make a simple apple pie, the humor of trying to take the whole chicken or cow with you, the silliness of trying to get cinnamon from under the nose of a sleeping leopard, or milk from a "polite cow". The wild parachute jump and the frantic readying of ingredients is followed by the ridiculous way the story nearly starts over and then abruptly stops. Finally, there is the exuberance of the plantation people and the wild pie-eating party attended by the cow, chicken, dog and cat!!

Humor isn't so much taught as caught and this is a good way to present "the funny story".

Language: Repetition

The author uses the element of repetition in *How to Make an Apple Pie.* The use of the line, "unless, of course, the market is closed," is echoed at the end of the story, "but if the market happens to be closed." Casually ask your student if he remembers any lines that were used more than once. Briefly point out that this is another way to create interest in a story. Perhaps someday you will discover the use of repetition in his stories.

Language: Vocabulary

ingredients	The individual parts that make up a mixture, such as the butter, eggs, apples, etc. for the pie.
superb	Something superb is wonderful.
locate	To locate something is to find it.
elegant	If something is elegant it is rich and luxurious.
coax, persuade	To try to get something done by using encouraging words or arguments.
native	Native trees are trees that have always grown in a place, not those brought in from somewhere else.
plantation	A plantation is a large farm, usually in the southern United States.

Language: Drama - Pantomime

It might be fun to act out the pages where the girl mills, grinds, boils, persuades, milks, churns, slices, mixes, bakes and even invites and eats. You could explain **pantomime** (acting without words or sounds). Have your student try it, or try the drama together and help him with actions he doesn't know.

Art: Street Scenes

You'll find a double-page picture of a street scene at the beginning of the story and again at the end. The first pages with illustrations show more of the left hand side of the street and the last scene pages show the rest of the street. The flag on the post office may help your student recognize this continuation. Find the book shop on the left side of the first picture and the locksmith and bakery on the right side of the "end of story" picture.

Call attention to the different roof lines, the different colors of each shop, the signs, the active people and the animals and flowers in the windows. (Explain that people often live above their shops.) Notice the actions of the lady holding her hat, the flag waving and the dog racing.

Take a piece of white legal size paper. Fold a third of it toward the middle on the right hand side. Open the paper and have your student draw a street scene using simple square and rectangular buildings over the full width of the open paper. Have him include any people, etc. he'd like.

When the drawing is complete, fold the right side back toward the middle to hide part of the street and open it again to see all of the street. Mention that the artist of *How to Make an Apple Pie* used the continuing town (over four pages) to bring the feeling of movement and unity to her story.

Art: Humor in Art

The story's last picture is a hilarious pie-eating extravaganza. Ask your student how the illustrator was able to show the children having such a good time? Some answers might include: lots of action, feet in air, hair flying back, reaching across the table, checkered napkins everywhere and a dog balancing a plate on his nose. See if your student comments on the chicken on the table or the cow that was invited to the party! Be sure to point out the author's use of a riot of primary, active, bright colors.

Art: Contrast

The blaze of color at the pie-eating party pictured with reds, oranges, blues, greens and the use of black, is in sharp contrast to the large expanse of white table cloth. If your student recognizes this concept, have him draw a picture where there is dark color next to very light color. Let him see how this technique makes a strong statement. It helps makes objects stand out clearly.

Math: Subtraction

Subtraction surfaces in *How To Make an Apple Pie* when the girl visits Vermont to pick apples."Pick eight rosy apples from the top of the tree. Give one to the chicken, one to the cow, and eat one yourself. That leaves five for the pie." Use this scenario to make apple subtraction math cards for learning and review. Math facts can be fun when they are tied to a story. Creative story problem scenarios could include the cow eating too many apples (choose your own numbers) and the chicken deciding she doesn't want one after all.

Math: Liquid and Dry Measure

How to Make an Apple Pie is a great story to introduce basic measuring and cooking skills. After using a plastic measuring cup to measure water (1 whole cup, 1/2 cup, 1/4 cup, etc.), and a metal cup to measure flour (don't forget to demonstrate drawing a knife over the top to level it), try cooking something together. Apple pie would be perfect, but anything requiring remembering the ingredients and measuring would be fun: Jello®, applesauce, macaroni and cheese. On a subsequent day, you could teach fractional addition: 1/2 cup + 1/2 cup =1 whole cup, etc.

Included in the cooking segment of these lessons is a chance for a memory game. Ask how many of the apple pie ingredients your student can remember. Remind him to recall the countries and the pictures for help.

Science: Salt and Evaporation

Salt, a mineral used since ancient times to flavor and preserve food, is a combination of the elements sodium (Na) and chlorine (Cl). NaCl is the chemical symbol for salt. The source of all salt, even the underground deposits, is salt water from seas and salt lakes.

See how salt can be derived from salt water by the process of evaporation. Place two cups of water in a shallow pan and dissolve 1/4 cup of salt in it. Allow the water to stand (in the sun is faster) until the water evaporates. Talk about the process of evaporation. See the salt left behind!

Science: Fresh Food for Health

Taking the cow along was the girl's attempt to insure the "freshest possible results." At the sugar cane plantation the girl flew home, so that the ingredients would not spoil. This is a chance to briefly explain that we should not leave milk and meat sitting out in the heat. Microscopic bacteria cause these foods to change and become dangerous for us to eat. These lessons can be expanded if your student seems interested.

GRANDFATHER'S JOURNEY

Title: Grandfather's Journey
Author: Allen Say
Illustrator: Allen Say
Copyright: 1993
Award: Caldecott for 1994
Summary: A young man understands his Grandfather's love for both his own
                home and a foreign land.

Social Studies: Family Relationships

Grandfather's Journey spans four generations and ties each of them together. After
several readings, discuss your student's ancestors. Try to identify any interests that he
might have in common with them. Perhaps his grandfather enjoyed fishing too, or her
grandmother also collected sea shells, etc. As the story points out on the last page, we
"know" someone better if we find that we share a common experience.

Social Studies: Geography

Find the island of Japan on the map (you'll recall there is already a story disk on
the map from *A Pair of Red Clogs*). This is where the "journey" begins. From Japan, the
grandfather takes a steamship to the New World. (Your student might remember discussing steam-powered machines and transportation from *Mike Mulligan and His Steam
Shovel*). Make a disk for the Pacific Ocean, which grandfather crosses, using the blank
story disks. Talk about how your student would feel if he did not see any land for three
weeks. It is hard to imagine. You might put the story disk for *Grandfather's Journey* on
California, the place he liked the best. You could also use a blank disk to make a marker
for the continent of North America. Explain what a continent is and that the North
American continent includes Canada, the United States, Mexico and Central America.
With your older student discuss the seven continents: North America, South America,
Europe, Asia, Australia, Antarctica and Africa. Locate each on your map. You may wish to
use blank story disks from the Appendix to label each of the continents.

In order to cross North America, many modes of transportation were used: steam
train p. 7, riverboat also powered by steam p. 13, and walking. If you are keeping up your
list of ways to get from one place to another, begun while studying *The Glorious Flight*,
then add any additional methods that come to mind: subway, scuba diving, etc.

This story portrays a love of traveling, a love of seeing things never before imagined and never thinking of returning home until Grandfather remembers his childhood. Yet this same story also emphasizes the value of one's birthplace and one's own country. It is a love that sooner or later calls us and requires our response.

Discuss with your student different places that each of you may have lived. Remember your favorite things about those places and any things that were not so good. Recalling and retaining memories is a skill that gives a sense of value and unity to one's life. It is also a great help in creative writing, as more and more details of people, places and things are stored away in memory for us to draw upon later.

Social Studies: Culture of Japan

Grandfather's Journey begins with a picture of Grandfather in his native dress, a kimono. A **kimono** is a loose fitting outer garment with short, wide sleeves and a sash, worn by both men and women in Japan. Your student may remember this from the story *A Pair of Red Clogs.* Page 22 actually shows a pair of clogs! Page 21 shows an entire group of people wearing kimonos. Look for other examples of Japanese culture. Notice the mountains of Japan. They are pictured in many Japanese works of art. See if you can find some examples of Japanese ink drawings with mountains and share them with your student. Notice the fan held in the woman's hand on p.23. Often, an Oriental fan is decorated with painting. The house pictured appears to be a house with walls made of paper, a common construction in Japan. Notice the dark hair and the well groomed hair styles.

Social Studies: History - World War II

You can discuss as much or as little of World War II history as your student finds of interest. You may want to simply say that WWII involved most of the world's major countries and was fought between 1940 and 1945, with Japan, Germany and Italy eventually losing. Or, you may want to go into more detail. You can touch on the Japanese surprise attack on the United States Navy's Pacific base in Pearl Harbor, Hawaii (December 7, 1941), the Holocaust (Nazi German's plan of genocide which killed more than six million Jews), the allied invasion of Europe on D-Day (June 6, 1944), the first use of nuclear power in the bombing of Hiroshima and Nagasaki, Japan (August, 1945), etc. Use your judgment as teacher to determine whether your student is ready for additional, supplementary material.

Social Studies: Tolerance for Different Races and Cultures

Mention briefly that the grandfather is a reasonable and friendly man. He enjoys meeting all kinds of people. He probably learns a lot from them. Remember that the grandfather is a **foreigner** (from another country). Re-read p. 12 in *Grandfather's Journey.*

Language: Poetic Prose

The writing style used by Allen Say is extremely poetic. He paints particular pictures with his words alone. This is called **imagery**. Poetic prose also uses the poetic devices such as **simile**. Allen Say writes, "Bombs fell and ...scattered our lives like leaves in a storm." A simile is the comparison of two unlike things using the connecting words like, as, seems, etc. Lives scattered *like* leaves in a storm presents a particular vivid picture to the reader's mind and uses the simile or comparison to accomplish that imagery. Re-read the text with your student and find other examples of Say's use of simile.

In addition, the very sentence structure that Allen Says uses is not like the typical action stories that your student might read. It is contemplative, and poetic with a gentle rhythm or cadence. There are not very many words in this story, but each word seems especially chosen to touch the reader's emotions. Yet, this story is not a poem. It is, rather, prose writing that makes some use of poetic techniques and devices. This type of writing is often called **poetic prose**. Ask your student if he enjoys how this story is written. He may already be learning to appreciate different writing styles. Also, with your student practice thinking of some similes. (See also Simile, *Cranberry Thanksgiving*, *FIAR* Vol. 1, p.67)

Art: Reflections and Shadows

Page 6 shows the sun's reflection on the water. It reminds us of the reflections in the story *Ping*. Maybe your student will catch this point first, but if not it's a good chance for review. Page 13 pictures the reflection of the steamship in the water.

Allen Say gives us examples of shadows on pp. 5 and 24. The sun (light source) is coming from behind the boy. But on p. 7 the hat casts a shadow over part of his face showing that the light is coming from *above*. Continue to experiment with flashlights in a dark room using blocks or apples for objects. Let the student see for himself how holding the flashlight (light source) at different angles moves the shadows to new places.

Art: Medium, Color and Contrast

Illustrations for *Grandfather's Journey* are paintings in a water medium (like watercolor or acrylic, etc.). The colors in some pictures are rich like Grandfather's sweater on p. 18. Some are subdued such as as pp. 10 and 13, yet all are carefully rendered a realistically.The strength and solidity of these illustrations are partly due to **contrast**. Notice the white collar against the black coat on p.5, the pure white of the umbrella against the green on p. 15, the white river against the dark land on p.11, and the married couple on p. 23. Nearly every picture is a study in contrast. Together, find more examples of contrast and keep *Grandfather's Journey* in mind as a prime example this element of art.

To some extent, all people are artists. Before artists begin their work they think about what they want to draw or paint. They consider elements like **balance, contrast, color** and **action** (or the lack of action). Remind your student that he can make choices like these as he thinks about the kind of picture he'd like to draw or paint. Make a list of the elements of art that you have studied (**viewpoint, contrast, color, unity,** etc.) Find examples from magazine pictures. Choose one with strong contrast and another with extremely bright colors, etc., to illustrate the various elements. Keep these illustrated art words in a notebook or make a chart of them. Then when it is time for art these ideas will be easy to pull out and review.

Art: Symbolism - Every Picture Tells a Story

Illustrations can deepen the meaning of a story. On p. 10, ask your student why he thinks Allen Say used dark (deeply grayed) colors. Ask him how the picture makes him feel. The text says that Grandfather is bewildered which mean he is not used to such large buildings and factories and he is confused by them. Rather than using bright, clear colors, the artist uses dark gray color to symbolize the confusion and dirtiness of the big cities. Page 11 shows a white river on dark land. Ask your student why the illustrator might have chosen white for the water. (It is possible that he was using the color white as a symbol to stand for purity. The text reads,"Rivers as clear as the sky." So the white may represent clear, clean water.)

Art: Formal Style

Allen Say has painted illustrations that are carefully posed, much like strong formal family portraits. Traditional Japanese art is formal and stable. Formality is evident both because of the formal poses and the unusual way in which each illustration is centered or balanced. In nearly every illustration, the object of interest is near the center of the picture. With your student, contrast this style of painting with the paintings of other children's books. Look at the work of Ezra Jack Keats (*Snowy Day, Apartment 3*) or at Marjorie Priceman's *How to Make an Apple Pie and See the World*. In these books the person or object of interest is often to the left or right of center.Note also that there is very little action in Allen Say's illustrations–yet they are beautiful. Your student may come to appreciate the variety in the illustrations of Allen Say and Marjorie Priceman. He can enjoy them both and know that in his own art he has a *choice* of ways to present his subject.

Art: Intensity

Page 19 shows a good example of intensity. A lack of intensity can give the effect of distance by using less detail and less intense colors (grayed or lighter colors) for background subjects. Ask your student why the buildings look far away. How did the artist achieve this effect? Perhaps he will say that the colors are very light and there is not as much detail as the figures in the lower part of the picture. Add this element to your list of art techniques. Find an illustration in a magazine to paste beside the word **intensity** as a visual aid. Review these techniques now and then.

Art: Origami

On the title page of *Grandfather's Journey*, you will find a painting of an origami boat. **Origami** is the traditional Japanese art of folding paper into shapes and animals. The word comes from the Japanese word "ori," meaning folded and "kami," meaning paper. Traditionally, the folding was done with colored paper squares, but today origami artists use various shapes. Check your local library for a book on origami. Pick up several sheets of brightly colored paper at your local arts and crafts store or use brightly patterned wrapping paper. Have fun learning this traditional, Japanese art form with your student.

Math: Days in a Week, Weeks in a Month

Grandfather did not see land for three weeks when he was traveling from Japan to the New World. Ask your student how many days that is. If necessary, explain the number of days in a week and use blocks or marbles to make three groups of seven. Count the total number and the question will be answered. You may go on to teach weeks in a month if there is interest.

Math: Counting

Counting practice can be done with the smoke stacks on p. 10 or with the total number of people figures from the beginning to the end.

Science: Different Land Types

Grandfather's Journey includes a variety of land types: mountains, both in North America and in Japan, deserts with their wind and sand-eroded rock formations, farm-land and the rocky coastline of California. Discuss the characteristics of some of these various geographic land types or regions.

Science: Factory Pollution in Cities

Sometimes factories are run in such a way that the waste and smoke from them seriously harm the air and water nearby. Some companies try hard to keep this from happening. They try to protect the air and water so the people and animals and plants near the factory are not injured. Page 10 shows a city full of factories. You cannot tell how these factories are managed, but this is a chance to talk about the effects of responsibility and irresponsibility. Protecting our **environment** (the natural world around us) is good stewardship and is becoming an issue of the times.

Science: Biology - Birds

Grandfather kept birds to remind him of the place *"where he was not."* Ask your student if he has ever had a bird for a pet. Encourage older students to research the origin of various pet bird species. Where do canaries come from? Parakeets? Cockatiels? Parrots? What care is necessary for a caged bird? (Birds need food, water, toys, a cage that is large enough, gravel for grit.) What are the characteristics of birds? (Birds have wings, feathers, beaks and bills, most fly, most build nests, etc.) You may want to discuss that bats have wings and a platypus has a kind of bill, even though they are both mammals. Birds can be classified (grouped) in different ways: by size, habitat (the region where they live), egg color, feather color, type of food, size, etc. (Some birds eat seeds, others insects, etc.).

Title:	Cranberry Thanksgiving
Author:	Wende and Harry Devlin
Illustrator:	Wende and Harry Devlin
Copyright:	1971
Summary:	Maggie's grandmother learns not to judge a person solely by the smell of seaweed or lavender.

Social Studies: Geography - New England

Cranberry Thanksgiving showcases a New England cranberry bog. New England is also the setting of *Night of the Moonjellies, FIAR* Vol. 1, p. 109. New England, in the northeast section of the United States, includes the states of Maine, Vermont, New Hampshire, Massachusetts, Rhode Island and Connecticut. The coastal states (all except Vermont), are bordered by the Atlantic Ocean. Maine, New Hampshire and Vermont share a northern border with Canada.

New England is noted for its beautiful rural towns and villages, Colonial historic sites, maple syrup, cranberries, ship building and manufacturing, and fall color.

Ask your student if he's ever eaten cranberries at Thanksgiving. Did he like them? Has he ever had cranberry juice to drink? Where does he think cranberries come from? Has he ever seen cranberries growing?

Cranberries grow on an evergreen bush, in bogs and in damp areas beside streams in the cool regions of North America. They are harvested and marketed as fresh cranberries, as berries made into juice and jellies, and as the traditional Thanksgiving cranberry sauce.

Maggie's grandmother fumes, *"Oh, a lot of people would like to get that recipe, especially Maggie's clam-digging friend, Mr. Whiskers."* There is a reference to clams in the New England area in *Night of the Moonjellies,* where they eat fried clams and clam chowder. Another children's book that mentions clams and shows clam digging is Robert McCloskey's *One Morning in Maine.* Maine, of course, is a part of the New England region. Find the New England area on your map. Place the story disk there and consider clam chowder and a glass of cranberry-apple juice for lunch.

Social Studies: Relationships

Grandparents: Maggie lives with her grandmother. This is one of several stories you will read in the *Five In A Row* curriculum with that special relationship of a child to his grandparent. Have your student find out special facts about his grandparents (even if they are no longer living), such as their favorite foods, hobbies, places to visit, etc.

Nicknames: *"That wasn't his real name of course. It was Uriah Peabody, but Maggie had called him Mr. Whiskers ever since she could remember. Maggie was very fond of Mr. Whiskers."*

Nicknames are not one's legal or real name. They are made up, sometimes based on what a person does, like "Speedy" for a runner, or based on what they look like as in the case of Mr. Whiskers. See *The World Book Encyclopedia* under Names, nicknames.

Ask your student if he has a nickname. Do you remember a nickname you had when you were small? Share the most interesting nicknames you've ever heard.

Disagreeable people: Mr. Horace, the man who smells of lavender and carries a gold cane, is not what he appears to be. He is a thief. He is willing to take something that is not his just so he can make money. Mr. Horace is a disgrace and he is also tricky. He tricks Maggie's grandmother into revealing her recipe's hiding place.

Talk with your student about the people who sometimes don't tell the truth, who are tricky and who want something so badly they are willing to steal it. These kind of people are difficult to deal with, but there will always be some who are like this. Again, one of the things your student can do is to continue doing the right things himself and be willing to forgive the people who have wronged him.

Mr. Whiskers (and you *know* how much he wants the pie) models forgiveness valiantly, and with true character as he gives Mr. Horace the last piece!

Judging by appearance: Maggie's grandmother bases her feelings about Mr. Whiskers and Mr. Horace solely on their outward appearances. Mr. Whiskers seems to the grandmother to be less desirable because he does not smell of lavender (a plant used to scent soap) and because he does not carry a gold cane, which she considers fashionable.

While it may not be wrong to be careful about a person that may not look "right" to you, Maggie's grandmother had some clues to help her make a good judgment. Ask how Grandmother might have known what Mr. Whiskers was like. What clues did she have? Your student might infer that Mr. Whiskers has lived nearby for some time because Maggie has called him by his nickname ever since she could remember. Also, Maggie obviously likes him and he helps her with her chores. Grandmother has been able to observe him and he has given her no concrete reason to be worried. She just doesn't like the way he is dressed. Grandmother finds out that judging solely on looks can be deceptive.

Ask your student how the grandmother finds out this kind of judging is wrong? Does she change her mind about Mr. Whiskers? (Yes she does.)

Social Studies: History - Thanksgiving

There are many children's books explaining Thanksgiving, its origins, and traditions. Ask your student why he thinks people celebrate Thanksgiving and what the word "thanksgiving" means. Talk about the "first Thanksgiving" and the reasons why people continue to celebrate it. Ask him what he remembers about the way his family celebrates this holiday. What are the special things they do and the special foods they eat? Does his family go to church, have grandparents or other family over, or watch the Macy's Thanksgiving Day Parade and the football games? Maggie's grandmother, in *Cranberry Thanksgiving*, suggests they all sing "*We Gather Together*," a traditional Thanksgiving hymn. You'll find a copy of this classic song in the Appendix.

Each family has unique traditions that your student can begin to appreciate. It is also good for him to know that not everyone does things the way his family does them. Teaching loving tolerance for others and their traditions is a lesson in manners which should not be missed.

Holiday time is a good time to brush up on "fine manners." Remind your student that a soldier does not stand at attention *all* the time. In the same way your student can learn he has especially fine manners that are like standing at attention. He may not perform to the same degree all the time, but for special dinners the "at attention manners" may be in force. And a good soldier *can* stand at attention when necessary.

In *Cranberry Thanksgiving*, Maggie and her Grandmother know that sharing is an important part of Thanksgiving. It is not whether the spoons all match, but rather the careful preparations that make the day special. Through the decorations, food and most of all through people being together, we turn a common Thursday into a special holiday.

Molly's Pilgrim, a heart-warming story, links the Thanksgiving tradition to the Jewish feast Sukkos. Barbara Cohen writes of a girl named Molly who is cruelly teased by her classmates until they find the tradition of thanking God for the harvest began long ago with people like Molly and her family. Also, Amanda Bennett's *Thanksgiving: Unit Study Adventures* has marvelous information and suggestions for the study of Thanksgiving. Check curriculum supply catalogs for this valuable resource.

Language: Setting

The setting for *Cranberry Thanksgiving* is concise and well-done. The first page states: "She [Maggie} and her grandmother lived at the edge of a lonely cranberry bog in New England, and the winds were cold at the edge of the sea." The action of the story actually begins on the next page. Have your student imitate this introductory setting with characters and places of his own choosing. For example: "Darcy lived with his uncle at the foot of a pine-covered mountain in Canada, where the bears roamed the woods and the sky was clear."

Language: Repetition

Repetitions are found in the text of *Cranberry Thanksgiving*. Mr. Whiskers asks to sing *Sixteen Men on a Dead Man's Chest* (an old sea song about pirates) during the beginning of the dinner. Grandmother is horrified, but by the end of the story Grandmother repeats the idea by suggesting the same song, herself.

Another of Mr. Whiskers' requests is also repetitive. The rhythm (though not the words exactly) and the idea are repetitive. At the beginning of the dinner you read:

"How delicious!" said Maggie.
"How exquisite! said Mr. Horace.
"How about some more?" said Mr. Whiskers.

and then near the end of the story:

"How delicious, " said Maggie.
"How delightful," said Grandmother.
"How about another piece?" said Mr. Whiskers.

Now you know why it isn't strange at all that Mr. Whiskers always shows up when Grandmother takes down her great yellow bowl and all the good things that go into it. He doesn't want the recipe--he wants something to eat!!!

Language: Poetic Prose Description

"*Everything wa̲s̲ cooked with cri̲s̲p edge̲s̲ and tender ̲c̲enters̲.*" These words cause your mouth to water and are descriptive in a poetic way. Alliteration helps make the words *poetic* with the "s" sound occurring five time in this line. Remember, alliteration is the repeated *sound* of a certain letter, not the exact letter itself so the "c" also makes the same sound as "s".

Also there is a balance of the descriptive words, *crisp edges-tender centers*. Perhaps you and your student will remember these words each year at Thanksgiving, for poetic phrasing is memorable!

Language: Poetic Device - Onomatopoeia

The literary device where a word makes the sound of the same object (the "snarl" of the saw, or the" buzzing" of the bees) is onomatopoeia. In this story, the sounds of scuffling (*Crash--clumpity!)* is onomatopoeia.

Language: Layout of a Manuscript

In *Cranberry Thanksgiving*, the layout of the text of the story contains wonderful variety. The words are sometimes at the top of the page, sometimes at the bottom. Sometimes they are on each separate page and other times only on one page with the rest of the picture opposite. Ask your student to follow the print with his finger as you quick-ly turn each page. He may say the print is at the top, bottom, the left or right. Even if he cannot read, he can see that he might find printed words in different places on each page. If your student is older, he can note the differences and remember that the text and pictures of books can be laid out in many ways. If he decides at some point to write and illustrate his own book he will make these same choices.

Language: Vocabulary

aura   a faint smell

starch   A substance that can be used to make fabric stiff.

wilt(ed)   become damp and limp; also a synonym for defeated

dart(ed)   to move quickly from one place to another

turnips   Point out this root vegetable at the market

peer(ed)   to look intently at something

murmur(ed)   to speak in hushed tones and somewhat indistinctly.

exquisite   extremely wonderful and perfect

bog   a low lying damp or watery area

Language: Elements of a Good Story

Discuss the elements of a good story in relation to *Cranberry Thanksgiving*:

Setting: The setting appears on the first page.

Conflict: The conflict becomes is someone trying to steal the famous recipe?

Rising Action: The tension, or rising action builds with the question *which* is the thief Mr. Whiskers or Mr. Horace? At the dinner, Mr. Horace tricks Grandmother into revealing the recipe's hiding place.

Climax: The most exciting moment is *"Oh, he's got it!"* and *"It's Mr. Horace!"*

Denouement: (day new MAHN) The falling action or resolution occurs when Grandmother throws Mr. Horace out, and then forgives him and offers him pie. There is also final resolution between Grandmother and Mr. Whiskers when *she* offers to sing *Sixteen Men on a Dead Man's Chest*!!!

Language: Figurative Language - Simile

"Maggie darted about like a black-stockinged bird," we read on the first page. Maggie is not a bird, but the author compares her to one. A **simile** is a **comparison** of two unlike things using the connective word **like** or **as**, etc.

In this simile, we see Maggie with long, bent, black-stockinged legs like the picture of the sea bird. The word, "darting", which often describes a bird, is used in describing the actions of Maggie.

Using similes in writing adds to the descriptive process and creates pictures in your mind of what the author see and wants you to see.

Have your student practice creating similes. Encourage him to imagine how soft or loud something is. Someday he may find similes useful in his own stories and poems.

The slipper was as soft *as*_____. (the gentle breeze, etc.)

_____was **as** loud *as* fireworks. (The man's voice, etc.)

The cranberry bog was lonely *like*_____. (an empty seat beside you at the movies., etc.)

The fire seemed cheerful *like* _____. (warm soup on a cold night.)

_____was as homey *as*_____. (The dulcimer music / gooseberry pie.)

Art: Partial View

Ask your student if he likes the picture where Maggie is peeking out the door at the recipe robber. This unusual half-face is an interesting painting to try to imitate. Take some symmetrical object, a toy animal or a ball, and put a large book or piece of cardboard in front of it to block half the view. Try drawing this "half-object." Don't forget to include in the drawing what it is that is blocking the view. Maggie's half-face would not have been so interesting without the balance of the door on the other side.

Art: Light and Dark

Contrast the picture where Mr. Whiskers is helping Maggie with her chores to the picture where Mr. Whiskers is chasing Mr. Horace around the tree. Flip back and forth, looking at each picture. Ask your student what the illustrators do to make the first picture look like day and the second picture to look like night. (The artists use brighter yellows in the "chores" picture, and less yellow, except for the windows along with more dark blues and purples in the "night" picture.) Try using dark blues and dark purples to make night scenes and remember that sources of light can be the moon, stars, lighted windows, lightning, and fires, etc.

Art: Warm Palette and Silhouettes

Wende and Harry Devlin paint these pictures using a warm palette (warm yellows, oranges, reds, browns and teal blues and greens with yellow added), in keeping with the subject of Thanksgiving; a day of family togetherness and warmth. This warm color theme reaches its climax at the hearth fire scene as Maggie's family and friends eat the pie. Long a favorite illustration of children, this silhouetted picture draws you into the room and practically puts a piece of pie in your lap!

The contrast of the white collars and cuffs (ask your student what these remind him of; perhaps the Pilgrims) to the black silhouettes is striking. The glow of the fire is just right for the end of the Thanksgiving dinner.

A silhouette (SIL o ette) is the dark outline of a person or object shown against a lighter background. There is no detail in the two-dimensional figure and it is usually done entirely in black. The white cuff and collar are the exception to a typical silhouette. Using a strong light and an easel (or board) with white paper, teacher and student may draw silhouettes of each other, and other interesting objects in profile. Be sure to use the word "profile" and explain what it means. Again, this information may not fully grasped now but this introduction of ideas helps your student's retention later.

Math: Measuring Skills

Review what you learned in previous lessons about measuring skills. Then add more difficulty to it. For instance, if you introduced cups and half cups, now use quarter cups and eighth cups. Explain the equivalents: two quarter cups make a half cup, etc. Try using third cups and also make use of measuring spoons. Then use the skills to make Grandmother's Famous Cranberry Bread. You can find the recipe on the back cover of the book. Your student might enjoy making this recipe each year and establishing a Thanksgiving family tradition.

Science: Seasons

The United States celebration of Thanksgiving takes place at the end of fall, and just before winter in the areas of the country with four distinct seasons. See if your student remembers the seasons and can name them and tell some characteristics about each one. If not, just talk about fall and the special things you associate with that season. (Rainy weather, harvesting crops, falling colored leaves, cool weather, school beginning, bluish-purple clouds, crisp apples, bonfires, Labor Day, squirrels hiding nuts, birds flying south, etc.)

Science: Starch

Starch is a substance found in the seeds of corn, rice, beans, etc. and in the stems, roots and tubers of tapioca, potatoes and arrowroot. There are different processes by which starch is removed and it has many uses. (See **Starch** in *The World Book Encyc-*

lopedia.) Two of the common household uses of starch are to thicken soups, etc., for which we use cornstarch and arrowroot, and to make ironed clothes stiff and smooth.

When the story says, "...*the starch seemed to leave Mr. Horace,*" the picture shows him crumpled in his clothing, but he seems to be crumpled in spirit, too. You can demonstrate starching a handkerchief and ironing it. When your student has seen and felt what starch does for fabric, take a squirt bottle of water and let him lightly spray the cloth. It should "wilt" quite nicely for him, and give a wonderful visual picture of "*the starch coming out of Mr. Horace!*" Then talk about "wilting inside", that terrible feeling of knowing that one has done wrong, of being found out, and being shunned by people. It doesn't seem as if being deceptive is worth the emotional consequences!

Iodine test for starch: Place a drop of medicinal iodine on bread, potato, fruit, carrot, flour, and orange juice. If the item turns dark blue/black there is starch present. Try the test on your laundry starch or spray a puddle of spray starch and try a drop of iodine there, testing for the presence of starch.

Begin a list of methods of testing for certain substances and add to it as you come across more. For instance, a method of testing for acid/bases is the litmus paper. There are many such tests that your student will encounter as he progresses through school. Therefore, keeping a list makes an easy review. Place the list in the science section of your student's notebook.

Science: Chemistry - Leavening - Chemical Reaction

Explain that when you bake, you need an ingredient that causes bread, cornbread, quickbreads, cakes and cookies to rise. Show your student an uncooked cake and ask him if he would like the cake if it stayed flat in the pan.

One of the things a cook might use for leavening (rising agent) is baking soda. Explain that another ingredient in the batter will react with the soda. This reaction will cause gas bubbles that make the cake rise. The second ingredient can be buttermilk, lemon juice, yogurt or vinegar. All of these are acidic and react with the alkaline soda to form gas. Have your student measure (whatever quantity you name) fresh baking soda into a bowl and set it in the sink. Then have him add some buttermilk, yogurt, lemon juice or vinegar and see if a chemical reaction takes place. It should form bubbles and possibly run over the edge of the bowl. (For your older student you can explain that the chemical reaction is releasing **carbon dioxide** gas bubbles.)

A chemical reaction is different from a mixture. In *Clown of God, FIAR* Vol. 1, p. 94, there is a science lesson about mixtures. Mixtures occur when several compounds mix together, but each remains chemically separate, held together physically by the liquid, like vegetables in a pot of soup. A chemical reaction, on the other hand, allows two or more compounds to combine and form one or more **new compounds**, different from the initial ingredients, like the chemical reaction that takes place when an acidic liquid is added to baking soda.

ANOTHER CELEBRATED DANCING BEAR

Title: Another Celebrated Dancing Bear
Author: Gladys Scheffrin-Falk
Illustrator: Barbara Garrison
Copyright: 1991

Summary: Envy and jealousy are thwarted by a true friend who shares his time and expertise.

Social Studies: Geography and Culture

Russia covers a large area. It has geographic extremes including cold regions (Siberia), high mountains, grassy plains and forests. Known for its caviar (a salty relish made from sturgeon or salmon roe/eggs), wheat and cotton, you can also find tigers, camels and reindeer in Russia! If you've ever heard of lemmings, you will find them there too. Russia is also known for its love of the arts. For **centuries** (groups of 100 years) they have produced **fine ballet** (such as the Bolshoi Ballet Company), excellent **authors** and **playwrights** (such as Chekov), **art and world-class music** (such as *The Nutcracker Suite,* written by Tchaikovsky). Collectors around the world prize Russian stacking dolls, called matrioshka, and intricately painted black lacquer Russian boxes. Consider listening to a little Tchaikovsky during lunch!

There are three cities mentioned in *Another Celebrated Dancing Bear.* Although this story was set many years ago in Czarist Russia (prior to the 1917 revolution), you can still visit those cities today; Minsk, St. Petersburg and Moscow. See if you can find them on a map. Now place your story disk on Russia.

From the time setting of this story when the czars ruled Russia, through the Communist takeover, the Russian people have not usually enjoyed the freedoms we have in the United States. You may want to discuss freedoms such as voting, free business enterprise, speech, religion, etc.

With your older student you may want to discuss Russia's czarist history, the communist revolution of 1917, the formation of the Soviet Union, the role of communism in world history, the cold war, the fall of communist Russia , etc. Students may also be interested in the Soviet Union's early lead in the "space race" with its cosmonauts.

Social Studies: Occupations

Ask your student if he knows what you mean when you say "someone's occupation". If necessary, explain that an occupation is a job. When the story begins what does Boris Bear do? What does Max do? Does your student think Boris doesn't like his occupation? What seems exciting about Max's job? Can people change their jobs or occupations? (Remember Mike Mulligan and Mary Anne from *Mike Mulligan and His Steam Shovel?*) What does Boris have to do to change jobs? (He has to learn how to dance and practice a lot.) Is it hard for him? (It is both hard and enjoyable.) Point out that for some people the job of caring for the animals would be the job they would most want to do. But Boris doesn't find the joy in that job that he discovers in dancing. Finding the right job is an important concept to think about.

Have your student think of occupations he might enjoy. Some students might have strong feelings about a particular occupation already.

You could use the topic of "occupations" for another long list. Add to this list whenever your student recognizes another type of job and if possible have him look for pictures to illustrate the list. Sometimes libraries have stacks of *used* magazines that are free, which have pictures of people engaged in various occupations.

(**Teacher's Note:** See *List Making*, FIAR Vol. 1, p. 7.)

Social Studies: Relationships - Hospitality

Max, seeing that his friend Boris is glum, greets him with a friendly wave and invites him in for tea. Max helps him off with his jacket and hangs it in the closet. He puts the samovar on to boil. Use this excellent story to discuss ways to be hospitable. Sometimes our friends may not be happy. How can we know how they are feeling? What are the clues? (They may be quiet, withdrawn, or have a sad countenance, etc.) How can we be encouraging? (Show concern, take time to listen, etc.) Talk about manners and being polite, respectful, and caring.

Boys and girls alike learn to be friendly, warm, and hospitable. You and your student can plan to invite someone to share a snack that you prepare together. Talk about the ways you will greet your guest and other forms of good manners.

Social Studies: Relationships

Another Celebrated Dancing Bear presents the issues of friendship, envy and jealousy. Talk about these kind of relationships and emotions. Discuss the fact that even with good friends or family there can be many different emotions: love, anger, envy, etc. Discuss positive ways to deal with them.

How does Max handle Boris' jealousy? He loves his friend and recognizes his sadness. Max is even willing to sacrifice his own time to help Boris learn to dance.

Language: Vocabulary

czar	an absolute ruler in Russia prior to the 1917 revolution
elegant	rich and luxurious
glum	a sad and miserable feeling
samovar	a metal urn with an internal heating tube, used in Russia for making tea
magnificent	fantastic, wonderful
jealous	anger with someone because of what they're like or what they have
audience	those watching a performance
marvelous	very good, wonderful
embraced	hugged
pyramid	in a triangle shape; (try to find the monkeys sitting in a pyramid)
comical	funny

Language: Characterization

"Boris was a heavy-footed brown bear whose heart was as soft as butter."
"Max–short for Maximovich–was taller than Boris and always seemed quite elegant."

Descriptive language, as in the example above, helps bring personality and life to the characters in this story. In order to learn to include such characterizations in his own writings, have your student do some descriptions patterned exactly after the above character sentence. For instance:
"Boris was a heavy-footed brown bear whose heart was as soft as butter," might become:

Sam was a lonely-hearted little boy whose clothes were as tattered as rags.

If it is too difficult for your student to think of an entire sentence, try doing one phrase at a time: "Boris was a heavy-footed brown bear..." could become Sam was a quick-thinking six-year-old.... And then, "whose heart was soft as butter," could be: whose hands were strong as steel, etc.

A sentence patterned after the descriptive "Max" sentence at he beginning of this lesson, might be:

Berni,–short for Bernedette–was faster than Jenny and always seemed quite active.

Creating descriptive phrases will help your student learn to bring personality and life to characters. These will eventually be used by your student in his own stories.

Language: Drama

Have your student act out the following action words from the story or act them out together:

applauded
bowed
beamed
drew near
giggling
chattering
mopping his brow
kicking (like the dance step)
leaping

Watch out, hilarity might be the result! Try to do a waltz together or imitate the "one--two--three--four"--glide forward then backward described in Boris' first lesson.

Language: Titles

In the story by Gladys Scheffrin-Falk, the title foreshadows the story. In the beginning of the story there is one celebrated dancing bear, and by the end of the story there are two celebrated dancing bears–**Another** *Celebrated Dancing Bear*!! Continue to remind your student that good titles require thought. Some are just names like *Madeline*, while some are questions like *Who Owns the Sun?* Others are inspiring like *The Glorious Flight* and some are mysterious like *Very Last First Time*. Most authors carefully consider a special title for each of their stories. Creative writing includes creative titles.

Art: Etchings

The explanation of the illustrations is found on the back of the title page. It tells in detail how etchings are done.

Let the student see some story books with watercolor paintings and help him recognize the differences between watercolor illustrations and these highly detailed line etchings of Barbara Garrison.

Art: Color

Another Celebrated Dancing Bear reveals the warmth and hospitality of a hearth on a winter's night. The illustrator has chosen a burnt umber ink, a brown with a touch of warmth, and added a watercolor overwash for the color portions. The colors (the warm red-orange of the vests, the scarves and the flowers) are nearly the color of a good hearth fire. Point out that the artist thought about it and chose colors to go along with the story; to help tell the story. Remind your student that *he* can make color choices to go along with what *he* is trying to say in *his* picture.

Art: Architecture

At the top of the first page there is a picture of a Russian skyline. Ask the student what he sees in in this picture that is not familiar to him. (Perhaps he sees unusual, spiral top "onion" turrets.) Try tracing several of the turrets from the Appendix. Cut them out and paste them on paper. Now, let your student draw rectangular buildings and towers beneath the turrets. In this way he can create his own Russian styled skyline.

Art: Noticing Detail

Reading *Another Celebrated Dancing Bear* for five days in a row will give your student a chance to notice more and more detail in the pictures. The illustration on the third page has a door knocker, a mail slot, and funny handles on the umbrellas. Barbara Garrison has included much small detail of Russian life and art in her etchings. Observe your student as he is able to point out new examples of illustration detail as you read the story each day.

Math: Hours on a Clock

Boris' first lessons were on Monday, Wednesdays, and Fridays from seven o'clock to eight. Take this opportunity to introduce the hours on a clock. Draw a very large circle on paper or cloth on the floor. Put in the numbers like the face of a clock. With your student, walk around the clock saying, "One o'clock, two o'clock, etc., as you step on the numbers. For your older student's advanced lesson ask how many hours are between one o'clock and five o'clock, etc.

Math: Seven Days in a Week

Discuss the seven days of the week and their names. How many days are there in a traditional modern American working week? How many days a week does your student think his grocery store is open? His library, post office, or farmer's market?

Science: Boiling Point and Freezing Point

Hospitable Max sets the samovar to boil. Explain that when heat is applied to water the molecules in the water begin to move around more rapidly. When the temperature of the water reaches a certain degree (212 degrees Fahrenheit or 100 degrees Celsius) the molecules move so fast they begin to "jump out of the pan" in the form of steam! This means the water is boiling. (Freezing point of water is 32 degrees Fahrenheit and 0 degrees Celsius). Remember these boiling and freezing point degrees are for water; other substances have different boiling and freezing points.

***Note**: After completing this lesson, you might enjoy reading *How the Tzar Drinks His Tea* by Benjamin Elkin. This is a wonderful story that shows more Russian architecture and provides further insights into Russian culture. It's a story too good to miss!

PAPA PICCOLO

Title: Papa Piccolo
Author: Carol Talley
Illustrator: Itoko Maeno
Copyright: 1992
Summary: A tomcat finds responsibilities, joys and satisfaction as he decides to
                adopt kittens!

Social Studies: Geography

Venice, Italy is the beautiful setting for *Papa Piccolo*. From the dedication page to the end of the story and even on the inside hard covers, you'll find information about Italy and scenes to help you remember the information. For the teacher: See if you can locate a copy of *Venice: Birth of a City* by Piero Ventura at your local library.

First, show your student where Italy is on the map and globe. Talk about the shape of the country. Many people say it looks like a tall boot with a high heel that appears to step into the Mediterranean Sea. Place the story disk for *Papa Piccolo* on Italy on your map or globe and refer to it each day you read the story.

Second, explain the streets of water and how the gondola boats take people where they need to go. Ask your student if he'd like to live where many of the streets are water. Maybe he can think of reasons why that would be fun and other reasons why it would not. (Where would you ride a bike or roller skate?)

Also, notice the architecture of the buildings, the bridges (pp. 25 and 28), the clothes of the people, and the bright colors (bright blues, yellows and reds) especially on the poles in the canals.

Social Studies: Foreign Language

There are Italian words and names used in *Papa Piccolo*. You might enjoy to learning a few Italian words. Use them frequently during the week. This builds vocabulary and intimacy as you share the experience. Some of the words are: bambini (infants, children) p. l2, caro mia (my precious dear) p. l8, Buon giorno (good morning) p. l0. Some of the Italian names in this story are: Caesar, Sophia, Luigi Barbaro, Zampeta's, and the Canal Tolentini. Your student will learn to associate the "sounds" of the names and words with

Italy as you use them and read them each day for five days. (As he did with the sounds of the French words and names in *The Glorious Flight, FIAR* Vol. 1, pp. 48-49.) In this way you will provide your student with an introduction to another interesting country.

Social Studies: Family Relations - Fatherhood

Papa Piccolo is about fatherhood. Ask your student to describe a father. Notice on pg. 8 that Papa knows what is best for the kittens though they aren't his own, and he sings lullabies to them. Even so, he doesn't want to be responsible for the kittens. What happens to change Papa's mind? (The kittens disappear and he finds himself worrying about them.) After the kittens return (notice the glad look on Papa's face, pg. 25) he teaches them what they need to know, pp. 25-27. How to eat spaghetti would be a very important thing to know in Italy!! You may want to use the list of what Papa taught the kittens for a memory exercise. See how many of the kittens' lessons your student can remember.

"And the three happy cats looked very much like a family." A family can be different combinations of people. Not every family can have both a mother and father and children. For example, if one parent dies, the remaining parent and children are still a family, etc. Love, discipline and sacrifice are needed for any family, and Papa provides well for his kittens. Page 18 states that love, care, time, patience and a sense of adventure are needed to raise a family.

On back of the title page is a dedication (above the striped poles): To Papas everywhere. (To *future* papas too?)

Social Studies: Flags

The inside front cover shows the flag of Italy and a smaller city flag of Venice. Using colored paper or watercolor make flags. Include the Italian flag and the long banner-type city flag of Venice. Fly them from the window or ceiling and celebrate the fun of learning about another country!

Social Studies: History - Marco Polo

What an enjoyable way to introduce the great explorer, Marco Polo! Marco Polo, an Italian was born in Venice. He traveled from Venice across Europe and Asia to China. He wrote about his adventures and let the people of Europe know about the wonders of China. Some of his descriptions were so amazing it was hard to believe. It is fitting that Papa names the kittens Marco and Polo. Like the explorer they live in Venice and they disappear on an adventure. Remind your older student that in writing stories, he may want to choose names that have a meaning beyond a particular character.

Social Studies: Human Relationships - the Homeless and Adoption

When Piccolo presents his plan to Sophia, she just laughs. "*Me? Take in two homeless kittens?*" This could present an opportunity to talk about actual homeless *people*. Why are they homeless? There are many different answers. What does the city or town do to help them? Talk about shelters, soup kitchens, food pantries, welfare and job hunting help, etc., available in cities and towns. Often domestic animals have no homes which sometimes creates problems. Talk about the ways people help in this area.

Another topic for discussion is adoption. Papa Piccolo was asked if he adopted the kittens. Explain adoption and talk about what's involved, how adoptive parents and children feel, etc.

Social Studies: Occupations on the Water

Page 22 tells of laundry barges that carry fresh linens to the hotels, garbage barges hauling away the cities refuse (trash), police motor boats on patrol, and water taxis transporting (carrying) eager tourists. Ask your student if he'd like to work on a boat that travels on the canals of Venice. Ask him to be on the lookout for laundry trucks, garbage trucks, police cars and taxis where *he* lives.

Language: Vocabulary

You may want to continue making index cards with these vocabulary words and pictures to illustrate them (drawn or from magazines, old National Geographics might show scenes from Italy). These cards can be filed in a box and reviewed every now and then. This will keep the words in mind and in use.

canal (p.5)   an artificial waterway for transportation (or irrigation)

trinket (p.6)   a trifle or a toy, a small piece of jewelry

sardine (p.6)   a small fish (cats love fish!!)

ledge (p.7)   small shelf sticking out from a window.

signora (p.7)   designates an Italian woman (like Mrs.)

situation (p.8)   condition or combination of circumstances

chime(ed) (p.9)   the striking of bells

carnival (p.11)   similar to a very small circus

regatta (p.29)   gondola race in Venice, term now used for any boat race

skiff, scow, barge and gondola (p.10)   kinds of boats

persistent (p.14)   will not give up; the kittens are persistent in following Papa

forlorn, glum (p.22) sad of face and expression like one's lost something special

gilded (p.29)   covered with gold

Language: Matching Descriptions

On p. 8 it says, "*And then Piccolo sang a little song he remembered from long ago-- about stardust and moonbeams and goldfish.*" Papa sang a lullaby (a bedtime song to help one sleep). Have your student think of some phrases that would put a dog to sleep. For instance, "I'll sing of bones and treats, slippers and silver-lighted dog houses," etc. What phrases could your student think of to put a butterfly to sleep, or a tree, or a eagle, etc.?

Language: Drama and Exercise

There is a lot of action vocabulary found in *Papa Piccolo*. Act out the words with body and facial gestures: strutting, sliding, and feasting, all from p. 12, wheeled, on p. 13, watching, begged and curled up, from p. 15, presented, on p. 18, gasped, on p. 19, groaned and leaped, on p. 20, and worried and glum, from p. 22. Occurring on various pages also find: tumbled, swung, curious, perched, awoke, prancing, ashamed and puzzled.

Language: Fable - The Fox and the Sour Grapes

Read the fable of the *Fox and Sour Grapes*. (Briefly, the fox sees grapes and longs for them, but when he discovers he cannot reach them from up high, he declares they are probably sour any way and he never wanted them at all.) Discuss the meaning of this fable. Ask your student to be ready to tell you when he hears a similar part in the story of Papa Piccolo. (p.12) Talk about people using the phrase, "That's sour grapes," in their every day speech. From now on, your student will understand the meaning of this phrase!

Art: Colors and Color Matching

From the title page (don't miss this picture!) to the end of the story, Itoko Maeno's beautiful watercolor paintings let you breathe the air of Italy and enjoy its sights, sounds, smells, and tastes. It almost seems as if you have been there! Maeno's use of colors (the bright colors of the Mediterranean) makes the story come alive. Ask your student to make a list of all the colors he sees in the double-page picture that follows the title page. Be prepared to help him with the names for the more difficult ones: aqua, pink, dark violet. Note all the colors that make up the water and others that make up the sky.

With a good set of watercolors (Prang® is a good brand), help your student try to match these colors by mixing his paints. He will learn that there are blues that have a touch of red in them and blues that have a little yellow mixed in. Begin with the simple color wheel (included in the Appendix). Show him how the red can have a *tiny* amount of yellow mixed in (not enough to be called orange) or the red can have a *small* amount of blue added and still be a "red".

An advanced concept for your older student is the idea of calling these colors **warm** and **cool** reds. If the red has a tiny amount of yellow added to it, it is called a *warm* red. Whereas, if the red has a touch of blue added to it, it it is called a *cool* red. The same warm-cool designation can apply to yellow, when red or blue is added in tiny amounts. And see the more advanced color wheel with its secondary colors, found in the Appendix.

Art: Advanced Color Theory - Complementary Colors

By using the second color wheel with its secondary colors, you can begin to teach colors and their complement. A color's compliment is sometimes called its opposite because they appear opposite one another on the color wheel.* Complementary colors are used to provide contrast and make vivid artistic statements. Maeno has made use of complementary colors on p. 7. Look on the color wheel and ask your student what is the opposite of red? (green) The artist has painted vivid red geraniums with dark green leaves. She could have chosen to paint pink geraniums but a stronger statement was made with the red and green. Look at the yellow and purple cushion on p. 30. There is a blue and orange picture on p. 20. Look for complementary colors in other paintings. (***Teacher Note**: Another aspect of complementary colors is that if you add equal amounts of each, as red and green, the color will become gray. Such an advanced concept isn't necessary for this lesson.)

Have your student look around him and notice colors people choose for their clothing. Sometimes a striking green shirt has a red tie to go with it or a beautiful yellow dress has a purple belt or scarf. People use colors and their opposites in decorating their homes inside and out. A red brick house could have green shutters, etc.

Art: Live Eyes-Highlights

The picture of Papa's face opposite the first words of the story shows a white dot in his eye. Point out to your student that this is an artist's technique. It makes the eyes look more alive. Have him look through the pages of the story and find other examples of this technique, then have him try a drawing or painting where he puts the light dot or highlight in the eye. He will discover that most of the time, rather than put white over other paint he will have to remember to *leave* that spot white. Perhaps he will notice the spot of light in the eyes of animals and people in other illustrations and magazines. Look for the highlight in good-quality photos of animals to see the "real thing" that the artist is copying.

Art: Creating the Illusion of Speed

Ask your student how the artist gave the impression the kittens are in a hurry on p.11. (The curving streaks of paint give the feeling that the kittens come from far away, swerve as they run and that they are moving so fast one can hardly see them.) Tightly tie an object (a patterned toy would be good) to the end of a 40 inch string. Now, twirl the string in a circle very quickly. Notice how the object is now just a blur and the patterns have disappeared. This is the effect Itoko Maeno was trying to accomplish in her painting of the kittens. Let your student know, he too, can try these speed lines and blurred images, in his own art, to show fast-moving objects and the paths from which they come.

Art: Use of Color for Light

On the page with the first words of the story, the artist has shown lighted windows. She has used yellow in differing shades to create the effect of light coming from the windows. The light is also reflected in the water (we studied water reflections in *Ping* and in *Grandfather's Journey*). Let your student try to paint a building with windows, using yellow for the effect of light. Remember, in order for the yellow to be effective, the surrounding scene must look at least somewhat dark.

Math: Counting

Count up the shoes on p. 17. If this picture shows only one of each pair, how many shoes would there be if each had its mate? If needed, line up a marble or domino to represent each shoe. Then put another beside it making groups of two. Count them all up. Talk about the concept of pairs and name things that come in pairs. (socks, pants [why?], scissors [why?], twins, shoes, earrings, etc.)

For high counting practice try counting all the windows from the beginning of the book to the end. (Notice that in Venice there are flowers boxes hanging in the windows–where else would their gardens be with streets of water and no yards?)

Science: Human Body - Peripheral Vision

On p. 11 Papa sees something "out of the corner of his eye." Talk about the concept of peripheral vision. Peripheral vision is the ability to see from the side while looking straight ahead. Have your student look straight ahead while you move a pencil from around behind his head toward the front. Let him determine when he can first see the pencil using his peripheral vision.

Science: Types and Breeds of Cats

The cat pictured on pp. 17- 18 is a Siamese. This is the name of a breed of cat. In any certain breed there are common characteristics like the blue eyes and patterns of coloring. The kittens, Papa and Caesar, represent different types of coloring found in many breeds. The kittens are called calico (black and orange spots) and tabby (striped).

VERY LAST FIRST TIME

Title: Very Last First Time
Author: Jan Andrews
Illustrator: Ian Wallace
Copyright: 1985
Summary: A little girl embarks on a long-awaited privilege and finds it wonderful, frightening, but in the end, rewarding.

Social Studies: Geography

Very Last First Time is set in Ungava Bay (pron. oon gay va bay, also pron. oon gah va), Northern Canada. Say Ungava Bay several times. Ask your student if he likes the sound of the name. Say it a few times together. This bay empties into the northern Atlantic Ocean, not far from the Arctic Ocean. Use blank story disks to label the Atlantic and Arctic Oceans. See if you can locate Ungava Bay on a map or globe. Place the story disk there. Point the disk out each day as you read the story, or see if your student can remember where to place it each day.

Ask your student what he can tell from the pictures and story about the land and climate of northern Canada. It is obviously cold, has jagged rocks, and it is close to the water. This area also has fur-bearing animals, scrub trees, and beautiful sunrises and sunsets. The land type is tundra (nearly level, treeless plains of the Arctic). The bay's *surface* freezes but as the deeper water recedes it leaves a space for the native people to walk on the bottom of the sea beneath the ice.

Social Studies: Inuit Culture

There is a great deal to be learned about the culture of the Inuit pronounced: (in you it) people by examining the story's illustrations, especially the first and second picture. The first picture shows, sled dogs, snow shoes, furs being stretched and dried, a church, and colorful clothes. The second picture reveals a modern kitchen, with running water and electricity (not found in the stereotypical igloos), cornflakes, perhaps oatmeal, and even paper towels. Ask your student if he thinks the kitchen looks inviting and enjoy his reasoning.

Talk about the cold temperatures and about the protection of fur boots and parkas (coats with fur hoods). The average temperature in Ungava Bay in January is negative 10 to negative 20 degrees Fahrenheit. The fur trimmed parkas are made from animal skins. These skins or hides are stretched on doors and the sides of houses. Discuss trapping and tanning, if there is interest. These are traditional activities of the Inuit. Also ask your student why Eva is searching for mussels. (The people of Ungava Bay eat mussels and they must enjoy them to work so hard for them.)

Social Studies: Family Relationships

What sorts of things does your student do with his mother? What sorts of things do children do with their mothers in other cultures? Find pictures, in books or magazines, of children doing various activities. Eva traditionally (ever since she could remember) had walked on at the bottom of the sea *with* her mother. It was what they did when they wanted to eat.

Talk about the enjoyment of doing things together. Ask your student if he thinks that when Eva was a very young girl, she was glad her mother hadn't just sent her off from their house to search for mussels by herself. When one is young it feels safe and good to be with your parents while doing difficult or new projects. Later when one is older there is be more desire to do some things by one's self.

Social Studies: Relationships - First-Time Experiences

Eva walks alone on the bottom of the sea for the first time in her life. Ask your student if he thinks Eva is excited. Does he think gathering food this way sounds like fun? Does he like to try things alone once in a while?

It is a special day when one is finally old enough to be allowed to do a certain new thing for the first time alone. When there has been a process of growth, a maturing, becoming ready for the next adventure or responsibility, then there is a desire for some independence. Discuss activities that your student has had to wait for: answering the phone, taking care of a pet, running an errand alone, etc. How many can your student think of? Was there something you remember waiting for? Was it difficult to wait? Share with each other. Is there something your student is presently waiting to do? (ride a horse alone, etc.)

Yonie Wondernose, written by Marguerite de Angeli is a story with a similar incident where seven year old Yonie is given responsibility. He then gets to do something he's been waiting for. It is a delightful story about Amish life on a farm.

Language: Story Writing - Good Titles

Discuss the importance of choosing a good title for a story. A creative title often draws you to a book. Jan Andrews thought carefully about the title for *Very Last First Time.* That title is a wonderfully mysterious invitation to the story. How can a first time be last? (because there is only one first time and after that there will never be for that particular thing another first time) Your student, too, can think carefully about the titles he chooses for his stories. Add "good titles" to your List of Choices Writers Can Make.

Language: Vocabulary and Drama

Act out the following words: dragging, shoveling, heaving, peering and fearfully peering, grinning, prying, scraping, singing, humming, scrambling, stumbling, groping, skipping, and squeezing. In acting out the words, your student will increase his vocabulary and remember more difficult words like prying, heaving (lifting or throwing something heavy), peering (looking very intently) and groping (reaching for something that cannot be clearly seen).

Art: Colors and Artistic Style

Ian Wallace used a full palette of colors. He uses warm oranges, yellows and browns, and also cool toned blues, greens and purples. Your student can see the difference in the picture of Eva first stepping into the ice hole. Her mother says,"Good luck," and the picture is predominately yellows and warm orange. Contrast with the picture of Eva coming out of the ice hole and squeezing her mother's hand. This picture while containing both warm and cool colors, is mostly made up of cool tones, purples and cool blues.

The illustrations are somewhat *pointillist* (made up of hundreds of tiny dots of paint) in artistic style. You'll also note the strong use of complementary color: purple with orange, blue with yellow, etc.

Art: Detail

Look for detail in Ian Wallace's paintings. Notice the picture behind the last picture of the story: Eva is sitting at a table eating mussels. She is reaping the rewards of her bravery. Discuss being brave, keeping calm, trying new things at the *right* time and feeling proud and happy with new accomplishments. Ask your student if he thinks these mussels that she gathered by herself taste better than any others? She looks very satisfied. (maybe because she was allowed the responsibility of helping to gather the family food)

See if your student can spot the shadow wolf, bear and seal sea monster in the picture where Eva has dropped into the ice hole and has lit her candle.

Math: Ordinal Numbers

If you have not already taught the Ordinal Numbers (numbers that name the order in which objects appear or are counted) use *Very Last First Time* to begin the instruction: Teach about first, second, third, etc. For practice use people in line at the water fountain, grocery store, etc. (Who is first? The man in green. Who is second? The little girl with the doll.) Also, line up a row of blocks and ask your student to hand you the third block or the fifth block, etc.

Math: Counting Practice

Count candles, barnacles, and mussels, etc.

Science: Safety and Crisis Thinking

Does Eva find out why younger children aren't allowed to go under the ice alone? Eva discovers that her mother has waited for a reason. Eva is old enough not to let panic (being very afraid) cause her to lose her way. If she let fear take over, she might forget the matches in her pocket. Discuss the importance of learning and practicing "crisis thinking."

CALM DOWN

DON'T PANIC

BE QUIET

THINK CAREFULLY!!

WHAT AM I SUPPOSED TO DO?

In following these rules of "crisis thinking" many times people will recall the significant information that will help them to safety. In calmness they will be able to make a good plan. There are many different situations in which "crisis thinking" can help: remembering where a door is, or to stay low in a smoke filled room, or knowing what to do in the first panicky moments of discovering that one is lost or separated from their party. Discuss dangerous predicaments and the safety rules that apply. (There are free picture brochures of safety tips at the fire stations and police stations.)

Science: Health - Dressing for Conditions

Discuss dressing for weather conditions. Dressing in shirt sleeves for 10 degree Fahrenheit weather is dangerous. So is wearing a parka in a 100 degree jungle. Learning to be more independent (doing things without being told) means learning to dress for the weather conditions of the day and even to pay attention to forecasts of changing weather. Draw (or find magazine pictures) for the proper dress in different weather conditions and in different seasons. Listen to weather forecasts together, and teach your student how to contact the weather number for current information.

Science: Subjects for Exploration

Very Last First Time provides an introduction to these topics:

tides   The water level on the beach, becomes more shallow as the tide goes out. The lowering tide allows Eva and her mother can walk under the ice. *Webster's Dictionary* defines *tide* as the alternate rise and fall of the surface of oceans, seas, and the bays, rivers, etc., connected with them, caused by the attraction of the moon and sun. The tide occurs twice in each 24 hours and 51 minutes. Discuss tides and tide pools (where often small animals are left behind in pools when the tide goes out). If there is interest find children's books on the topic.

biome   Biomes are large geographic areas having a similar climates including the plants and animals that live there. Some different types of biomes are: tundra, coniferous and deciduous forests, deserts and tropical rain forests. Ungava Bay is a tundra-type biome. (cold and without trees)

echo   An echo is the repeating of a sound produced by the reflection of sound waves from a surface. Talk about where you might hear an echo. Echoes are commonly heard where the sound waves are not absorbed but rather reflected, as in a cave, a long, empty hallway, in the mountains, etc. In *Very Last First Time* Eva's song echoes around under the ice. It sounds interesting to her so she sings louder.

ocean life   Eva sees the blue-black mussel shells, small shrimps and pinky-purple crabs that live at the ocean. These animals are shellfish. She also sees anemones and seaweed in wet, shiny heaps. There are tide pools left when the tide goes out. In these pools many ocean plants and animals can often be seen. Explore ocean life and make a poster or by drawing some of the subjects you've studied.

sea salt   Sea water contains salt. It makes swimming easier because the salt helps the swimmer float. The amount of salt is similar in every ocean because the waves cause a mixing action. Eva could smell the salt in the ocean air. Stir some salt into a small glass of hot water. Can you smell a smell like the sea? (Obviously, the ocean is not hot water, but the ocean spray does carry the scent of salt.)

Science: Simple Machines

Eva uses her knife as a **lever** (and the rocks or shell as a fulcrum) to pry the mussels off the rocks. Teach the use of simple machines and how they make life easier for us. Other simple machines include: the **inclined plane**, the **wheel and axle**, the **pulley**, the **screw** and the **wedge**. The wedge and the lever were studied in the lessons for *Who Owns the Sun? FIAR* Vol. 1, p. 41.

CLOWN OF GOD

Title: Clown of God
Author: Tomie dePaola
Illustrator: Tomie dePaola
Copyright: 1978
Summary: Clown of God is the retelling of an old legend, a story of a "gift for *the* Child."

Social Studies: Geography - Sorrento, Italy

Clown of God is set in Sorrento, Italy. Sorrento is an actual Italian city. Let your student know he could still visit there although it would not look the same as the early Renaissance setting of this story. Nor would the people be dressed in the same way, but he might still see a monastery and a Franciscan monk. Italy is the long, high heeled boot shaped country that appears (on a map) to hang down in the Mediterranean Sea. Using a map or globe, place your story disk on Italy.

Social Studies: Foreign Language - Italian

Review the Italian words previously studied from *Papa Piccolo, FIAR* Vol. 1 p.76. Add these Italian words and Italian names : Arrivederci (ah-reeva-dair-chee) means good bye, Grazie (grat-zee) means thank you, Signor (seen-your) denotes Mr., and Fine (Fee-nay) means the end. The names are Giovanni, Arlecchino, and Colombina.

When you say "good bye" to your student, when you end a book or activity, and whenever you say "thank you," say it in Italian!

Social Studies: Renaissance

The Renaissance was a period of time in history during the 1300s, 1400s, and 1500s. At this time there was a great revival of learning and art.

When teaching young students about subjects like the Renaissance, try using pictures of clothing, foods, and activities. Gather these and show them to your student and ask him what is different from the way we live today. Let him point out things that are different and then say, "There is a word we use for this time in history, when clothes, etc., were like you see here—it is **Renaissance** (Ren-ah-sahnce)." Let him enjoy the sound of that word and say it with him several times. Some students will not memorize now, but they will have been introduced to the pictures and the words--a good beginning!!

The Clown of God pictures the early years of the Renaissance. Notice the clothes, the lunch of bread, cheese and fruit, going to market with woven baskets, no shopping carts, being entertained by jugglers, traveling actors, etc., no television, movies or video recordings, and horse-drawn transportation.

Social Studies: Orphans

The story provides an opportunity to explain the term "orphan"– a child without mother or father. In this story Giovanni has no parents and no one at all to take care of him. Throughout history, due to plagues and wars, many children have been left alone. You can discuss the ways these children are cared for.

Arleta Richardson has written a series of books that tell of the **orphan train** in America called *Looking for Home* and *Whistle-Stop West*. The orphan trains took thousands of orphans from the America's eastern cities across the midwest to find new homes with rural families during the last half of the nineteenth century.

In the *Samantha* books of the American Girl Series, Samantha meets an orphan and befriends her. These are excellent read-aloud.

There is also a wonderful series about a family of children who run a farm and have countless adventures after having lost their parents. The stories read like the *Little House* books and are most enjoyable. The reader sees the children accept responsibility and keep a warm family life. These books are called the *Hannah's House* Series. They were written by Rhoda Wooldridge. The series includes: *Hannah's Brave Year, Hannah's House, Hannah's Flood, Hannah's Mill* and *Hannah's Choice. (*Available at libraries.*)*

Social Studies: Elderly

Giovanni grows from a child to an elderly man in the course of this story. In his case, the people do not show him respect nor do they feel any compassion or desire to help him. Discuss with your student the respect that is due older people. Sometimes older people need encouragement that they have value even if they cannot contribute in the same way that they have in the past. They can be recognized for the wisdom, skills and knowledge that they can pass on. Ask your student if he has any elderly friends and talk about them. Does your student have any grandparents that he sees regularly? Try one or more of these books that showcase older people and their relationship with a child: *Mrs. Katz and Tush* by Patricia Polacco, *Gramma's Walk* by Anna Grossnickel Hines, *Storm in the Night* by Mary Stolz, and *Uncle Jed's Barber Shop* by Margaree King Mitchell.

Social Studies: Thankfulness

Take the time to remind your student that there are many things for which to be thankful. By reading about people like Giovanni who had a hard life, the student may identify with certain aspects of life's difficulties, and yet realize that he has many things for which to be greatful. Make a list and illustrate it, or make a time line of the student's life and add all the events and people, etc., for which he is thankful.

Social Studies: Relationships - Difficult People

"*And wherever Giovanni went, the faces of the crowds would be all smiles, and the sound of laughter and cheers would ring through the towns.*" But as the years passed, people no longer stopped to watch and they did not respect the old clown who had entertained them. When he dropped "*the Sun in the heavens,*" they first laughed, and then threw vegetable and stones at him. Ask your student why the people acted this way. Discuss the fact that some people, thinking only of themselves, want to be amused. That is all that is important to them. Your student will meet people like that and it helps to understand why people act the way they do.

Wise people enjoy entertainment but also care about the people that entertain them. Discuss the fact that when someone is popular and then falls out of popularity they may experience a loss of self-worth. Having people who care can make a real difference. Is there someone your student knows that needs to be encouraged? Discuss the ways he might do that.

Social Studies: Occupations

From the very beginning of this story, Giovanni is happy because there is something wonderful he can do. In juggling, Giovanni finds a purpose (to entertain) and a way to make his living. And one day the monks even tell him that by doing what he is able to do he gives happiness to people and glory to God as well!

Discuss with your student that it is important to discover what things he can do. It is also important for people to know the value or contribution of their job. Giovanni said, "*I used to make people smile.*" Giovanni thought that seemed valuable. Here are some other careers and some of their possible values:

A newspaper man might say, "*I help the people know what is going on.*"

The cook: "*I feed people to make them healthy and to make them happy.*"

A house painter: "*I paint houses to make them beautiful.*"

Giovanni: "*I juggle to make people smile!*"

A doctor: "*I treat people to help them get well and to comfort them when they are sick.*"

An artist: "*I paint, etc., so that the beautiful and meaningful things can be preserved.*"

A farmer: "*I grow food so that people will have potatoes and corn to eat.*"

This is how I help the world; *this* is what I do!

Language: Legend

Legends are stories that sometimes have elements of truth but that have been embellished (made greater) by many additions which are not necessarily true. They sometimes glorify a person, or an event in which, a miracle happens.

In England, King Arthur has become a legend because many stories naming him have been handed down for generations. In America, men like Davy Crockett and Daniel Boone have reached epic legendary proportions.

According to Tomie dePaola, *The Clown of God* is an old French legend. Yet, the author says that following the tradition of story tellers, he adapted the story to the setting of which *he* was most familiar: Italy.

Language: Vocabulary

juggle	to toss several objects (more that two) in the air, keeping them moving in an arc (portion of a circle) until you want to stop
eggplant	a purple vegetable; Point out unusual vegetables at the market. However, you probably shouldn't try to juggle them!
zucchini	a vegetable; Have some on hand to display. Now, try juggling!
famous	well-known
arrangement	items grouped in a certain way
troupe	an artistic group of people; dancing or acting group who work together
maestro	an Italian word that means a master of any art
ragamuffin	a ragged person, young or old
companionship	being with people
torches	sticks that are on fire; Find the picture in the story.
violet	a bluish purple, a mixture of red and blue; Find the violet ball in the picture.
brothers (monks) (monastery)	monks in a monastery, a place where these men seek God as they live a cloistered (isolated) life; Find the picture of the monastery and one of the little brothers.

amazement	wonder
serious	without humor or silliness
magnificent	marvelous, wonderful, great

Language: Reading Comprehension

After reading the story, ask your student why Giovanni goes to the vegetable stand every day. (He goes so he will have objects to juggle.) What is the arrangement he makes with Signor Baptista? (Giovanni will juggle and draw a crowd. Signor Baptista knows the crowd will stop and buy his vegetables and fruit. In exchange for the help of drawing the crowd, the Signor's wife will feed Giovanni–a very good arrangement!)

It is helpful to know if your student is picking up the facts as you read a story. It is also good to notice if he is able to infer ideas from what you read to him. Be on the look out for ideas that are inferred. See if the student has understanding. Reading, ultimately, is more than just looking at the words and being able to say them. It is understanding the meaning of the words, sentences, paragraphs, and ideas that are inferred from the text. Reading often to your young student will have a positive effect on his reading readiness. (Your older student will enjoy hearing you read to him as well.)

Language: A Balanced Story

In *The Clown of God,* you find an exceedingly well-crafted tale. One of the literary devices Tomie dePaola used is **balance**. Notice the story beginning with Giovanni, the orphan, who is begging and who then meets the monks (little brothers). Toward the end of the story, Giovanni is begging again and happens upon the monastery, the very one the little brothers are from. The story beginning soon reveals Giovanni as a happy juggler and ends with him as happy juggler, doing what he was meant to do.

Try working together with your student to create your own story with balancing opening and closing scenes as Tomie dePaola has written in *The Clown of God.*

Language: Repetition

There are repetitive lines in *The Clown of God*. One series of repetitions is the order in which he throws up the colored balls. He throws a red ball, an orange ball, then a yellow ball, a green ball, blue ball, and violet ball. Finally Giovanni throws the Sun in the Heavens (the gold ball). This "order" of action is repeated as he juggles at the monastery.

There is a repetition of subject (rather than words) as Giovanni begins the story needing to beg for food, and is poor again at the story's end.

Language: Contrast

There is a contrast of emotion between Giovanni, the happy child juggler and the defeated old Giovanni. Can you and your student think of story ideas that would have great contrast of emotion or action? (For instance imagine a person who is very sleepy. Then something exciting happens. He is now completely awake! You might think of someone who appears quite fearful but something happens and they find they are brave. Or, imagine someone who boasts he can do something and finds out he cannot.) When you create story scenarios of this type you sharpen literary skills while exploring the world of emotions.

Language: Story Endings

What keeps the ending of this story from being *too* sad? How has the author accomplished this? (Giovanni is very old and has lived a hard life. It is a thrill to watch him put on his face and juggle better than he ever has before. It is also a shock to realize that he has given the performance everything he has left. Yet the miracle of the smile on the face of the child and the hand holding the golden ball inspires us and leaves us in awe.)

How a story ends is very important. Remember the Afterword in *Who Owns the Sun?* that helps ease the sorrow of the ending. Remind your older student that in crafting a story, he gets to choose an ending that will express the message he has to tell.

Art: Juggling

There is an art to juggling. There is a rhythm, a timing and a way of tossing by which Giovanni brings entertainment to the people. If you, or someone you know, can juggle, let your student see in person the wonder and excitement of this entertainment form. Let him try. If your student wants to learn and be great, then like Giovanni with his juggling and Lentil with his harmonica, he will discover that he must practice. If he decides to make a serious attempt to juggle, have him stand with his waist against a bed (so he doesn't have to bend over so often to pick up the balls) and situate himself with a plain, solid color wall behind the bed so there are no visual distractions. Try making him three small, round bean bags to practice with. (Don't stuff them too tight and they'll be easier to catch.)

If you should happen to go to a circus, be sure to watch for the jugglers!

Art: Medium and Style

Tomie dePaola has used pencil, ink and watercolor on hand-made watercolor paper to illustrate *The Clown of God.* His figures are flat and often in profile (seeing a face from the side). Notice the stylized trees; stylized, but not all the same. There is variety. Have your student try drawing, painting, or even modeling (with clay) some stylized trees like those in the drawings.

Art: Recalling Venice, Italy

Giovanni travels with the acting troupe. He then begins to perform on his own. Cheers ring through the towns. One of the towns he visits is Venice, Italy. Perhaps you have covered the lessons for *Papa Piccolo, FIAR* Vol.1, p. 76. If so, when reading *The*

Clown of God, give your student time to recognize for himself the picture of gondolas, the gondoliers, waterway streets, and striped poles. All of these sights appeared in the illustrations of *Papa Piccolo*. If your student doesn't recognize Venice share with him and compare these pictures with the illustrations from *Papa Piccolo*.

Art: Symbolic Detail

There is a picture of a dove on the title page. Opposite the first words of the story, "*Many, many years ago in Sorrento...*", the dove reappears. Find it in the picture where the discouraged old juggler washes off his face and goes back to begging. In this picture, the dove is hiding its head. The dove may symbolize (stand for) Giovanni's talent or his career, for it sits atop the stage on the title page and sits opposite a juggling ball on the next page. On the page where he gives up his career, it hides its head. Or it may just represent Giovanni's sorrow in losing his feeling of being valued (sense of self-worth). In any case, it is enjoyable to notice and appreciate such artistic detail.

Art: Architecture

The Clown of God provides marvelous architectural examples to be introduced, and enjoyed. Eventually, your student will begin to recognize familiar styles in books and actual buildings around him. Note the massive stone bridge with people walking on top and the shops above the bridge. (There is a terrific book for children on bridges: *The Bridge Book* by Polly Carter. This book is fun to read, has understandable illustrations and shows an example of the kind of bridge found in *The Clown of God*.)

Notice the columns with the different types of statues at the top. Your older student might enjoy researching architecture and the various columns of Venice. If he is interested he could also use an encyclopedia (see Architecture) to introduce himself to the classical types of columns (Doric, Ionic and Corinthian, etc.). He may want to discover when and where they originated. If he is observant, he will probably see many examples of these three column types in the architecture of his town or city. Maybe he will also notice columns with animal figures on top of them as illustrated in this story.

The arches pictured throughout the story are Roman arches. These are rounded at the top, rather than pointed like Gothic arches. Even the arches in the monastery are the Roman type, including the massive arched doors and the windows.

The round window on the front of the monastery is often seen in churches today. Notice that you can see part of this round window from the inside of the monastery as well as the outside. Ask your student if he has seen this type of window and have him be looking for them (especially on churches). (**Note:** There is an informative book on windows called *Let There Be Light* by James Cross Giblin. This book tells the history of windows and contains many fascinating facts that can be shared from time to time with your student. An memorable learning experience for the teacher!)

Art: Appreciation - Sequencing

The double-sided picture where Giovani is juggling at the monastery is a thrill to view. The reader nearly holds his breath as across four identical arched spaces Giovanni juggles first six balls, then all seven, higher than he has ever juggled before! These pictures appear in a sequence, much like a cartoon strip. The repetition of the arches provides a rhythm for the juggling.

Math: Grouping and Pre-Multiplication

Use the picture of Giovani juggling three eggplants. Ask your student how many different groups of eggplants Giovanni can juggle if Signor Baptista has twenty-one eggplants in his vegetable stand. Take twenty-one blocks, marbles, etc. if necessary, and make groups of three until they are all accounted for. Now count the groups. (There should be seven.)

Gear this lesson to the level of your older student. At this time you may want to introduce the "x" multiplication sign. You can say, "You will be learning a faster way to know how many groups of 3 there are in 21. By using the 'times' sign, we learn the number fact that 7 groups of 3 (7x3) equals 21. It is always the same. That's why we call it a fact."

Continue using the picture of Giovani juggling four oranges, five torches, and seven balls to make more grouping lessons for your young student. For your older student who is learning his multiplication tables, have him make multiplication fact flash cards and decorate them with the colored balls that Giovanni juggles.

Math: Counting Practice

For simple counting practice, have your student count the total number of colored balls pictured in the story. For higher counting, have him count all the objects that Giovanni juggles. You can also count trees or people.

Science: Mixtures - Cooking

Giovani was happy to have his bowl of soup from Signor Baptista's wife. He probably didn't think about the fact that his soup was a mixture. In chemistry, the term "mixture" means a combination of substances held together by physical, rather than chemical, means. An easy way to explain this term is to make soup. Make soup by taking meat, water, and spices, and cooking them gently together creating a soup "mixture". Have your student look at the soup. He will see soup, but he still will be able to recognize carrots, potatoes. This is because the ingredients are still there, but they are now held together in the liquid. If your young student finds this lesson hard to grasp, never fear, he will recognize the terms as he is re-introduced to the topic at a later time, and the soup making is fun!

Science: Aging

As people get older, many have a harder time seeing as clearly as they used to, or hearing the faint sounds they once did. They may also have difficulty doing things with their hands and fingers that they could once easily accomplish. What they do have, that they did not when they were younger, is experience in many areas of life and the wisdom (the accumulation of insight, knowledge and experience) which comes from living life. When a student is reminded of the importance of respect for the elderly people he knows, an avenue is opened for friendships that can be enriching indeed.

An advanced science lesson would be to research the elderly and the reasons for the aging process.

For your young student, it is enough for him to be aware that an older person might not be able to hear as well as he can, or that they might drop something, wear dentures, etc. By discussing these ideas with your student he will begin to have compassion and tolerance born of knowledge, rather than ridicule born of ignorance and surprise.

STORM IN THE NIGHT

Title:	Storm in the Night
Author:	Mary Stolz
Illustrator:	Pat Cummings
Copyright:	1988
Award:	1988 ALA Booklist Children's Editors' Choice
	1989 Coretta Scott King Honor Book for Illustration
Summary:	Grandfather addresses Thomas' fear of thunderstorms by vulnerably relating a story of his own childhood.

Social Studies: Relationships

Thomas and his grandfather have a close relationship. What things does your student see that show how Thomas and his grandfather feel about one another? Perhaps your student will mention some of the following reasons that he feels they are close:

(1.) Thomas loves his grandfather's stories. He loves them so much he asks for them again and again. His grandfather explains things to him. He sits close to his grandfather in the pictures. Thomas admires his grandfather for being able to tell "a truth like *that*".

(2.) Grandfather loves Thomas. He spends time with him and helps him admit his fear by telling Thomas his own vulnerable story. Grandfather is not judgmental or preachy regarding Thomas' fears, but says, "*Perfectly natural.*"

Does your student have someone with whom he shares stories and spends time? Have him describe the relationship. He might say something like, "I spend the weekends with my grandfather. He makes me fried potatoes and we go for long walks."

Social Studies: Emotions - Fear

Thomas says, "*I'm* not afraid of *anything.*" Ask your student if he thinks this might be a boast and why? (Most everyone will admit to fearing *some* things.)

Grandfather helps Thomas know that all people are afraid of something, some time, and that it's "ok" to admit it. He also teaches that fears can be overcome. Sometimes people are afraid of the dark, storms, or of experiences that are new or unfamiliar. Discuss with your student things that have made *you* feel afraid, and ask him if there is something that bothers him.

Grandfather tells in his story that he forgot that his parents had gone out for an hour or so, because he was afraid. As he said, "...fear does strange things to people...makes them forget everything but how afraid they are." This is why learning and practicing Crisis Thinking (studied in *Very Last First Time,* Science-Health and Safety, *FIAR*, Vol. 1, p. 85) is important.

This story has a happy ending when the electricity is restored. Is it Thomas' hand that willingly turned off the lights when Thomas and his grandfather go to bed?

Language: Contrast

Look at the contrast in descriptive words between the opening lines of the story, describing the fury of the storm, and the lines near the end when "the storm was spent."

Beginning:	**Ending:**
Thunder like mountains blowing up	mutterings of thunder
Lightning licking the navy-blue sky	flickers of lightning
Rain streaming down the windows	little patter of rain babbling in the downspouts

Let your student hear the contrast and try to imitate a series of descriptions with a contrasting series. For instance:

Horses, galloping like rifle fire	horses stepping quietly
Snorting, sides heaving	breathing softly
Screaming, wildly	whinnying gently.

Language: Punctuation - Italics

There are several examples of using italics for emphasis. (If you did the Italics lesson in *The Glorious Flight*, *FIAR* Vol. 1, p. 49, you have already introduced, to your student, the use of this punctuation for the names of boats and ships.) In *Storm in the Night,* italics have been used to show great emphasis. In a handwritten story, these words would be underlined. Examples from the story:

"Were there *automobiles!*"

"*I'm* not afraid of *anything.*"

"I want to own a *tiger!*"

Help your student recognize that italics is a different type of print from the rest of the text. Your student will be able to tell the difference in the types of print even if he cannot yet read. Mention that one use of this type of print is to *emphasize* the word that is italicized. Make sure you read the italicized word with voice emphasis each day. An older student may want to experiment with using one or two emphasized (underlined or *italicized)* words in a story.

Language: Punctuation - Quotation Marks

Storm in the Night is an unusual children's picture storybook because of the amount of dialogue it contains. Try reading Thomas' dialogue in a certain voice and Grandfather's dialogue with a different voice. Then your student can easily follow who is doing the talking. Because of the great amount of dialogue, this story may be better appreciated the second or third reading. (Explain that dialogue is conversation; when two or more people are talking to one another.*)*

When you read dialogue in a book you can see that each time that a person speaks, what he says is placed inside quotation marks. Show your student how quotation marks look. When one person stops speaking and someone else begins, a new paragraph is formed. This is to help the reader understand *what* is being said and to know for sure *who* said it.

Let your young student dictate to you a simple story with some dialogue. Show him how you are using quotation marks. Let your older student try a story with dialogue, too.

Language: Vocabulary

mandarin   in this story—orange colored; comes from mandarin oranges which are small, spicy sweet oranges with a bright orange peel. If you can find canned mandarin oranges, enjoy some for a snack while you read.

bough   a branch of a tree

errand   something that one goes to do; Mom ran an errand when she went to the store to get milk.

Language: Poetic Device - Onomatopoeia

Mary Stolz writes a prose story that has poetic elements. One such element is the use of **onomatopoeia** (ona-mata-pee-uh); a word that makes the sound of the object when you say it. The clock striking: ping, ping, ping-a-ling; or ticktickticktickety; or bong, bong, bong, BONG! would be examples of onomatopoeia. (See *Glorious Flight, FIAR* Vol. 1, p. 50, Poetic Device - Onomatopoeia)

Remind your student that using onomatopoeia is like writing in sound effects and adds variety to his stories. Have him try a short story using some sound effects.

Language: Poetic Device - Personification

Personification is a poetic device that gives human attributes to non-human things. Speaking of the heavy rain, Mary Stolz described it as "whooping wildly" and "brandishing branches." There is also a phrase, "horns...hollered," and a clock that was "excited." (See *Mike Mulligan and His Steam Shovel, FIAR* Vol. 1, p. 44, poetic device: **personification**.) With your student look and listen for other examples of personification in stories.

Language: Poetic Device - Simile

Mary Stolz has included a striking **simile** (sim-uh-lee) in this story. Simile is a statement that one thing is like another, using the connective *like, as,* etc. *"That man was seven feet tall and had a face like a crack in the ice."* Like a crack in the ice. What does that kind of face look like? Ask your student to draw his impression. Similes are used to create greater avenues of description by likening one thing to another. Remember Thomas' voice, *like* a penny whistle, while Grandfather's was described as being *like* a tuba? Even though their voices are not musical instruments, by knowing the characteristics of those instruments, you now have a poetic description of their voices.

Language: Setting and Scenes

The setting for *Storm in the Night* is Thomas' grandfather's house. But, within this setting, the scene changes from the inside of the house to the outside and finally back inside once more. This variety of scene, even within a very small setting, is interesting and something worth pointing out to your student.

The setting itself, and when to change the scenes, are choices a writer can make. Writing is like being in charge, like being the boss. All the choices for a story are waiting to be made. Remind your student *he* can make those choices when *he* writes a story.

Art: Medium

Pat Cummings has used oil or acrylic paint to illustrate *Storm in the Night*. Notice the white rain slashes on the title page. Look for them on the other pages. Observe the white highlights around people and objects and watch for brush strokes (esecially visible in Grandfather's sweater when Ringo the cat jumps onto Thomas' lap) in many of the pictures.

Oils or acrylic paints allow white to be applied *over* color, unlike water color where you usually leave, without paint, any spaces you wish to be white . If you have access to acrylic paints, a canvas, a medium wide brush and a very long, thin scroll brush, try with your student, painting a dark blue background in different intensities (strengths) of the same blue. This is accomplished by adding varying small amounts of white to the same blue. Let it dry and use the scroller with white to try the rain slash marks, like the title page. Try some dots and splashes too! If it isn't possible to work in this medium, a simple lesson can be accomplished with the sharp edge of white chalk on dark navy blue paper. Try to use dark blues for night (rather than black) as Pat Cummings did in this story.

Art: Expressing Darkness and Light

With the exception of the last half-page of the story, *Storm in the Night* takes place in the dark! How does the artist show the darkness of the night? (The illustrator uses blues of many intensities with white and yellow highlights.)

There are different sources of light. The sun is our primary source of light but it does not appear in this story. However, there *is* light in the story. Where does it come from? Ask your student if he knows. Three sources of light in this story are lightning, the woodstove fire and electric light bulbs. Pat Cummings has painted the light from the lightning as white. Notice the pictures where the highlights are white. You know the lightning is flashing. She has portrayed the woodstove firelight with yellow and orange. Find the pictures lit by the light of the woodstove. There is a yellow glow is from the electric light bulb on the last page of the story. On the page where the boy asked his grandfather if there were automobiles when he was a boy, notice how light the room is. Compare this illustration with the picture without the flash of lightning, where the boy said his grandfather knew more stories than a book.

Pat Cummings also uses white outlines in many of the pictures to contrast with the dark blue night.

Art: Reflections

There are several examples of reflections in this story. There is the reflection of the cat in the window where the boy says, "I like cats. I want to own a tiger!" There is a reflection of the grandfather (when he was a boy) in the window as he tells his story. Reflections of faces are difficult, but an adventurous art student can try a picture that includes a reflection. Remember, reflections come from smooth, shiny surfaces. Windows, mirrors, eyeglasses, a shiny kettle, water, a pond, or a raindrop can all reflect images.

Art: Facial Expressions

In the picture opposite the words, *"There were clocks,"* Thomas is looking out the window. He is looking sideways. You can tell because the iris of his eye is over to the side and you can see more of the white of his eye that when he is looking toward the reader. It is very easy to draw faces with the characters looking different directions. Let your student try drawing faces with eyes like the ones shown at the bottom of p. 100.

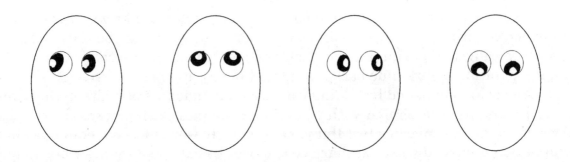

Art: Contrast

The last illustration shows a half-yellow and half-black picture. The contrast is used by the artist to make a dramatic statement. When you want to make a dramatic statement, you use complementary colors (or colors close to them). These are sometimes called "opposites" on the color wheel. In this case, the yellow makes a strong contrast to the bluish black. A dark blue next to the bluish black would have been less striking.

Art: Profiles

A profile is a view of a face from the side. The cover illustration is an excellent example of faces in profile. You can see the cat's face, then Thomas' face and finally his grandfather's face placed in profile from smallest to largest. This illustration is truly a triumph of balance, repetition and beauty. Take a toy animal or doll with a definite profile. Let your student try drawing it, and if possible, try repeating the pattern at an angle across the page. Or find pictures of faces in profile in old magazines and cut them out. Let your student paste them on paper in a repetitive pattern.

Math: Geometry - Quilt

Grandfather tells the story of the night he heard the thunder and hid under the bed. Look at the quilt on the bed. Ask your student what shapes make up the quilt pattern. Maybe he will recognize the triangles (three-sided polygons whose angles add up to 180 degrees). These look like equilateral (equal-sided) triangles. The center is a small, white circle surrounded by a yellow pentagon (five equal-sided polygon). Try making the some equilateral triangles and pentagon with your geo-board. (See *The Rag Coat, FIAR* Vol. 1, p. 35, instructions for making geo-board in the Mathematics: Geometric Shapes lesson.)

Science: Sources of Light

Make a list of the light sources that you can think of: sun, moon with reflected light from the sun, stars, lightning, fire, lightning bugs, moonjellies and other sea creatures, flashlights, light bulbs, neon tubes, etc. Discuss that a very small amount of light can dispel darkness. Try to find a very dark room. Give your eyes time to adjust to the darkness. Light a match or switch on a tiny flashlight. Notice with your student how very bright the room becomes with just a small amount of light.

Science: Safety

Your student will enjoy learning about the safety precautions he can make use of during a storm. He might also like setting up a "storm survival kit." (There are free brochures on weather and what to do in case of severe weather at your local police station or television weather station.) A "storm survival kit" could consist of a flashlight (keep fresh batteries, especially during storm seasons), or candles and matches. Also, a small first aid kit, a transistor radio with fresh batteries in order to hear severe weather reports, could be included as well. Ask your student if there is anything else he would like to include in the kit. Help him decide on a special place to keep the kit. He needs to remember where the storm kit is kept and practice finding it in the dark! Taking these steps might one day prevent panic, should your student find himself home alone. Remember Crisis Thinking (See *Very Last First Time*, Safety-Crisis Thinking, *FIAR* Vol. 1, p. 85) and practice.

You could role-play this situation: Your student is home alone. He hears a loud clap of thunder, the lights go out, and two more very loud thunder-boomers split the air. It sounds as if the house will be next! What should he do? (Calm Down, Don't Panic, Be Quiet, Think Carefully, What Am I Supposed to Do?) Maybe he will say after the above steps, "I need to make my way to the place where we keep the Storm Kit and get the flashlight. If the radio says I need to get to a place of safety, then I know where to go. Otherwise, I will enjoy the storm, knowing that I have everything I need and my parents will be home soon." This kind of training gives your student a feeling of security and responsibility and can prevent many traumatic experiences. Use it for other safety procedures: fire drills, swimming precautions, earthquake or hurricane warnings, etc.

Science: Five Senses

Thomas discovers that he can hear better in the dark and also that his sense of smell is enhanced. Ask your student if he thinks this is so and why. (Grandfather explains that your senses are sharpened when you're not trying to use all five at once.) Try sitting in a dark room and listen carefully for sounds that you have not noticed before. It may seem as if each sense is magnified in isolation (used alone.) Go outside. Cover your eyes tightly and concentrate on various smells. You and your student will both be surprised at what you discover.

Science: Aging

Thomas tries to imagine Grandfather as a boy, but it is difficult. List the things he finds different between his aging Grandfather and himself. (Thomas' voice is like a whistle while Grandfather's is like a tuba. Thomas doesn't have a beard, but Grandfather has one, and Thomas is short, while Grandfather is much taller.) Add to the list things your student observes about elderly people, such as being retired, doing volunteer work, walking with a cane, having trouble hearing, having grandchildren visit, or having skin that is wrinkled. Remind him though that many people have begun new successful careers and accomplished wonderful things even in their mature years. Just one example of this is Grandma Moses (Anna Mary Robertson Moses) who began her famous painting career while she was in her seventies!

Find several photographs showing the same person through various ages. Perhaps the student has several photographs of a grandmother or grandfather as children, young adults and as senior citizens. You might also locate photographs of movie stars from forty years ago and their current photos today. Let your student carefully compare the images, noting the changes which occur in the aging process. (The dark hair has turned white, the skin has wrinkled, teeth may have been replaced by dentures, etc.) You'll both find this a fascinating project! If you can, go back and look at the paintings in *Grandfather's Journey*, and notice the changes in Grandfather.

Science: Clouds

There are different cloud types. Begin to teach your student what they are and the weather they may bring. He may enjoy making use of this type of information throughout his life.

Clouds that are in flat layers are stratus clouds (strato means "in layers or sheets"). Stratus clouds can be associated with rainy weather. Cumulus clouds are white, piled up, billowy masses (cumulo means "heap or pile"). They often appear on sunny days and signal fair weather. Cirrus clouds are delicate, curly, thin upper altitude clouds. They are made of ice crystals. (cirro means "curl"). These high clouds signal cold air at high altitudes. Nimbus clouds are gray and dark, often bringing rain (nimbo means "rain").

A combination of cumulus and nimbus clouds are called cumulonimbus clouds, which tower in columns. These clouds often bring violent thunderstorms.

Science: Thunderstorms

Thunderstorms are characterized by high winds, lightning, heavy rains and sometimes hail. They are caused when warm, moist air meets cool, dryer air. Although most common in the spring, thunderstorms can occur any time of year; even in winter when they become *thunder-snows!*

If you have thunderstorms in your part of the country, try to experience a thunderstorm with your student and discuss it while you watch and listen.

Encourage your student to smell the air during a thunderstorm, and again afterwards. Have him try it with his eyes closed! Sometimes people can smell an approaching rain shower before it arrives. This is because small water molecules (not drops but more like a spray) are carried ahead by the wind before the actual storm begins!

Title: Katy and the Big Snow
Author: Virginia Lee Burton
Illustrator: Virginia Lee Burton
Copyright: 1943
Category: Classic
Summary: Katy becomes a heroine as she finally gets her chance to work and
              fulfills her responsibilities

Social Studies: Running a City

Even though *Katy and the Big Snow* could, at first glance, seem like a dated book, your student can still learn a great deal about machines and how they work from it. In fact this story contains a wealth of learning opportunities from map skills to art lessons. You'll find lessons on how a city operates and how the people perform their responsibilities. In addition your student may be as fascinated with the illustrations as readers were in 1943. *Katy* has been loved for generations, and will continue to delight the next generation, as well.

Katy and the Big Snow gives a look at city life and the departments necessary to keep that life moving along. On pp. 6-7, you will find that in the margins Virginia Burton has already illustrated thirty places in Geoppolis. Talk about the different buildings and occupations and how each contributes to the city. Match these numbered pictures to the numbers on the map in the center of the page. Can your student name other types of businesses and occupations necessary to running a city?

Virginia Burton named the town Geoppolis. Ask your older student if that name sounds like any word he knows. (*geography, geology,* etc.) The author symbolized city life everywhere with this name because "Geo" means earth, and "polis" means a city-state in ancient Greece. Thus, Burton's Geoppolis stands for a typical city anywhere on earth.

With your student, make an imaginary city out of blocks or boxes or just a draw a large map. Think up a good name for it. Include the businesses and buildings that your student thinks are important. If he forgets critical services such as doctor's offices or fire stations, etc., ask him if he thinks it would be good to include them. Explain the consequences of not having that business or service available. You'd hate to have to drive to another city for your mail or groceries!

If you have an old white bed sheet, you could draw your student's own town using magic markers for the streets, etc. Remember that markers can bleed through the fabric and take protective measures.

Social Studies: Relationships - Responsibilities

Each building or farm represented in Geoppolis has people running it. Each of those people has a job to do in order to keep the town running smoothly. What if the fireman decided not to work today and a house burned down? What if the mailman just didn't feel like delivering the mail? Each person has a responsibility to do his work faithfully (on time) and honestly. If he fails—other people will suffer.

Ask your student what would happen if Katy does not clear the snow. (The schools, factories, stores, railroad station, and airport will have to close. The mail cannot be delivered, the police will not be able to protect the city and the telephone, electric and water lines cannot be repaired. The doctor will not reach his patients and the Fire Department will be helpless.) Katy has a large responsibility.

Ask your student if he has responsibilities. Does he do them faithfully, sometimes heroically, like Katy? If he does, he needs to know that it makes a difference to those around him, just as Katy's contribution made a difference in Geoppolis.

Social Studies: City - Street Signs

Pages 4-5 show street signs in the margin border. Some of these signs are still used today, but there are some that need to be added. Check your police station for brochures with pictures of the signs. Get two brochures, and make a chart with one. Have your student place the other in his notebook. Many of our signs today are symbolic signs. Teach these signs to your student, along with the reasons for the picture symbols. He will enjoy pointing them out as he notices them along the road. You may want to make miniature signs. You could place them on sticks with clay bases and use them in the town you made in the lesson "Social Studies: Running a City, p.104."

Social Studies: Map Skills - Directions

An introduction to points of the compass and map skills flow naturally from the story *Katy and the Big Snow*.

The most basic lesson begins with the introduction to the directions: north, south, east and west. Most maps show north at the top. To make sure of orientation, always check the map's legend. The legend will point out which direction north is on that particular map. In *Katy*, the compass points are at an angle. This orientation renders north to be in the two o'clock position. If your student is interested, have him follow this slanted compass view on pp. 24, 26, 28 and 30.

If possible, obtain a compass for your student to examine. Explain the directions. (The metallic needle aligns itself with the magnetic poles of the earth, and points toward north.) Make a simple treasure hunt with an enjoyable object at the end; perhaps a new book, or lunch, etc. Help your student follow a series of clues based on turning certain directions. The directions might start on the west side of the building and instruct your student to go south to the corner of the yard, and then to turn east, etc.

Together, draw a map of your student's neighborhood. Decide which compass direction will be at the top. Make a legend to inform others. Draw it from an aerial (bird's-eye) view. In addition, talk about which way your student's home faces. Sometimes point out the direction you are traveling when on outings. Keep in mind that the sun and moon can help determine direction, also.

Language: Meet the Character - Katy

A great amount of description is given about Katy on p. 1. Not only does the text of the story tell about Katy, but Virginia Lee Burton has graphically shown ten facts about her in the border pictures of that page. Burton said she often put details in the margins or on the end papers, because they were too weighty for the body of the text and, yet, children had assured her that they were often their favorite point of interest.

Ask your student to list what he remembers about Katy from p. 1. Then complete the list by re-reading the page. (Katy is red. She is a crawler tractor with 55 horses of power and she runs by a diesel engine. She has five speeds forward, two backward and can turn around in the same place. Katy has country shoes, city shoes, and a hydraulic lift system for her blades. She also has a bulldozer and a snow plow. She is very beautiful, big and strong, and Katy can do a lot of things.) Each day, after reading, see if your student can remember a few more of the characteristics of Katy. Developing a good memory is a lifetime benefit.

Language: Literary Device - Personification

Katy's character is portrayed with human qualities by the use of the literary device called **personification**. Giving human qualities to non-human objects, animals or things is called personification. In *Katy and the Big Snow,* the author has given Katy a feminine pronoun "she" and writes that she *"likes to work–the harder and tougher the job, the better she likes it."* Also, Burton used dialogue. When Katy is asked to help, she speaks as a person, and she even gets tired but won't stop. She "hurries" to work and then she goes home to rest. Dialogue, emotions, physical weariness, and heroism (not stopping even when tired) are human attributes. When the author presents Katy in this way, it is as if she has human personality. With your student, try writing a story giving human characteristics to a non-human object.

Language: Vocabulary

bulldozer	a piece of earth-moving equipment
steam roller	a piece of road maintenance equipment that presses the road flat; this equipment today is no longer steam-powered but rather it is usually powered by diesel engines

drizzle	light rain that may last for several hours
water main	underground pipes that carry water
emergency	a situation that calls for immediate attention
three alarm fire	a serious fire that requires three different fire stations to respond
patient	a person under the care of a doctor

Art: Detail

Virginia Lee Burton has illustrated this story with exquisite detail. This detail is expressed in bright color, exciting action, oodles of information, and courageous personality.

Color Detail: The colors, especially the red, green and yellow, make a bright display for "getting the work done" throughout the story. The dark aqua-blue represents the blizzard day as on pp. 14-15, making the white snow stand out in contrast.

Detailed Action: The details of action are continuous throughout the story because the city life is active with many people working all the time. Katy works too. The final rush to plow the big snow beginning on p. 16 and reaching its busiest climax on p. 33 shows the action mounting and moving across the page rapidly. Trace the path of Katy's plowing through the pages, but especially pp. 34-35. Have your student rapidly move his finger along Katy's paths. Perhaps he may be able to *feel* the action the illustrator drew as the art of the story translates into *emotion* for the reader.

Detailed Personality: The personality of Katy comes from the headlights, made to look like eyes. (See the cover picture and find other examples in the story.) It also comes from her "nose to the grindstone" method of working and her comments of "Chug! Chug! Chug!" as if she just *has* to complete her work, which Burton draws into the pictures. Let your student try to draw a picture of something not human drawn with human characteristics. (Example: a tea pot with a happy face, a chair with a face and arms that hug, a flower dressed up, etc.)

Math: Counting

Your student can count the number of telephone poles on the cover, the number of horses on p. 1, the number of bulldozers on p. 2, etc. There is a great variety of counting practice possible in the numerous illustrations of *Katy and the Big Snow*.

Math: Grouping and Counting by Fives

To represent horsepower, Burton has drawn eleven groups of five horses each. You can give your student fifty-five marbles, pennies or blocks (or horses if you have them!)

and have him put them into groups of five each. He will be able to see that eleven groups of five make the original fifty-five objects.

Explain to your older student that he can also count items more quickly when he learns to count by fives. If there is great interest, introduce the method of counting by fives.

Science: Weather - Patterns

Explain that weather is not the same from year to year. You can have several years in a row with heavy snows and then several years without a heavy snow. There are flood years, drought (dry) years and normal years. If your older student is interested in weather, help him research a given area. Learn what kind of weather patterns there have been for that area in the past one hundred years. You'll find this sort of information available at the Weather Bureau or your local library.

Your young student might enjoy keeping a weather calendar with weather picture symbols for each day. Weather symbols could include: sun, rain, clouds, snow, wind, fog, etc. Help him keep it for a month and note the resulting weather information. For example, there may have been six sunny days, two days of rain, ..., etc.

NIGHT OF THE
MOONJELLIES

Title: Night of the Moonjellies
Author: Mark Shasha
Illustrator: Mark Shasha
Copyright: 1992
Award: A Marion Vannet Ridgway Award winner
Summary: A seven year old boy helps his grandma at her restaurant and she
                shares a secret with him.

Social Studies: Geography - New England

Mark Shasha has written a book set in a New England town by the sea. Find the states that make up New England: Maine, Vermont, New Hampshire, Massachusetts, Rhode Island, and Connecticut. There are many good children's picture books showing the culture and life of New England. Many libraries also have video selections about the Northeast United States. Place your story disk on New England. If you desire, find on a map and label the Atlantic Ocean with one of the blank story disks.

You may want to discuss why this area is called *New England*. The Pilgrims came from England and began to settle in new land. Because they had come from England, they called this new land, *New* England.

Social Studies: Introduction to Running a Small Business

In the story *Night of the Moonjellies,* a seven-year-old boy helps out his relatives in their small family-owned restaurant business. These family run small businesses are sometimes called Mom and Pop businesses.

What sorts of qualities would be important in running a small restaurant? (Keeping a clean establishment, maintaining healthy food preparations, being friendly, honest, dependable owners, and having knowledge of business affairs.) Activities, with which owners of small businesses must deal, include: purchasing supplies, paying bills (electricity, water, hired help, building payments, supply costs, insurance), cooking and cleaning up, waiting on customers, paying quarterly and monthly taxes, etc. Many small business owners enjoy the satisfaction of being the boss. However, the responsibilities can be overwhelming for first-time business owners.

Ask your student to think about a type of business he might like to run and why. Let him imagine being boss. Ask him what kind of people he would hire, and where he would like to have his business. (a mall, a corner shop and maybe live upstairs above it, in his own home, etc.) Does he think he would enjoy working at *his* business as much as the boy in this story?

Social Studies: Responsibility

Does your student think this seven-year-old boy takes care of the responsibility he is given? What is he asked to do? (He is to fill the catsup, mustard, and relish containers. He is in charge of refilling the straw and napkin holders, and cleaning up the yard [inferred from the illustrations]. He also must stack the hamburgers between pieces of waxed paper, crank open the umbrellas, help with the onion rings, and with drying and putting away the pots and pans.) Do you think he does his job carefully and cheerfully? Can you tell from the pictures? Do you think he *likes* the responsibility? Have your student share the type of responsibilities *he* has at home.

Social Studies: Life Near the Sea

Life near the sea (in *Moonjellies* this means the Atlantic Ocean off coast of New England) has waves and tides, fried clams and clam chowder, along with lobsters and lobster rolls. There are lots of other animals near the ocean like starfish, periwinkles, and jellyfish (called moon- jelly fish), sea gulls, and lots of sand. There are many kinds of boats including fishing boats, lobster boats, and sail boats. The place to repair boats and buy supplies is called a marina. The air by the seas smells like a mixture of salt and seaweed. There are outdoor shops and stands with many things for sale.

Have you or your student ever been "by the sea"? Share your experiences and memories. If you happen to live near the sea, share stories and memories about a trip to the desert or country instead.

Language: Contrast

Re-read the portion of the story where the customers are crowding and the radios blaring, horns beeping, etc. Then re-read the description of the thousands of moonjellies stretched along the sea in every direction, as the boy and his grandma stand on the deck and watch the shimmering sea. Look carefully at the accompanying pictures. These scenarios are opposite of each other: one rather frenzied and one more peaceful.* The variety of scene provides an overall contrast of feeling for the story. Talk about contrast in color like black against white and then about the **contrast in** these **words and feelings** of the story. Let your student try to write a paragraph with contrasting elements such as joy and sadness, or slowness and speed, or heat and cold, etc.

*Ask your student which scene he appreciates most. Some people love the hustle and bustle of a city with the accompanying noises, sights and smells, while others enjoy a more peaceful country place with the beauty of nature all around them. Either of these preferences are valid, but they also demonstrate contrast!

Language: Punctuation-Italics

The names of ships and boats are underlined in handwriting and set in *italics* in printed type. The fisherman in the story that transports the moonjelly to its home has a boat named the *Periwinkle*. Show your student the place in the story where they go to meet the fisherman and his boat. Let him see that the word *Periwinkle* is set in different type. Even if he cannot read the word, he can still recognize that the type is different.

You may have already seen the name of a boat in italics in the story *The Glorious Flight*. (Obviously, the names of books are also in italics.)

Language: First Person Point of View

Night of the Moonjellies is written in first person point of view. That means that the boy writes about himself and those he knows. We see only from his eyes and he uses words like "I", "me", and "mine." Try writing a story using the first-person point of view.

Language: Vocabulary

marina   a dock for mooring boats and having supplies, sometimes a service station

pier   a structure to land and/or tie up boats or ships

moonjellies   common jellyfish found on the coasts of the Atlantic and the Pacific Oceans

Language: Make a List

See how many of the food items mentioned in *Night of the Moonjellies* your student can remember. Make a list and draw pictures next to the words. Let your student add more words to the list each time you re-read the story to him.

Art: Medium - Pastels

Pastels are a kind of chalk-like crayon used in drawing. The depth of color is achieved by layering the color and building up the layers. Often when rough textured paper is used you can see the bumpiness of the paper showing through the chalk pigment. Textured paper can then become part of the overall effect of the drawing. If you have access, try some experiments with pastels. The ocean water on the cover picture would be fun to try to match " in effect" though you may not have the same colors. These short, choppy strokes with lots of colors are worth trying. Oil pastels are easier for children to work with since they don't smear as much as chalk pastels. They have long been a favorite of children because of their intense colors. (**Note:** Make sure your student understands the two uses of the word "*pastel.*" It can refer to a type of color palette characterized by soft, gentle colors, and it can also refer to a type of artistic medium made of either dry chalks or oil chalks in stick form.) **CAUTION**: Teacher supervision is necessary with pastels. Your student should not put pastel chalks in his the mouth and he should wash his hands after using them.

Art: Layout

Illustrators and publishers choose how the text and the pictures in a book will be laid out before the book goes to the printer. In *Night of the Moonjellies,* the decision was made to have a single drawing span both pages of the text from the edge of the left side to the edge of the right side. In this story, there are very wide rectangular-shaped pictures.

Write and illustrate (perhaps even bind*) a small book. Decide if you want a picture under every page of text or one picture spanning two pages of text, as in *Moonjellies.* Decide what medium (watercolors, pastel, pencil, crayon, etc.) you will use. Decide if the pictures will be humorous (as in *How to Make an Apple Pie and See the World* or serious as in Grandfather's Journey)? Remind your student *he* is the author-illustrator. He gets to make the choices!

*Valerie Bendt's *Creating Books with Children* is a wonderful resource. Along with valuable suggestions to help children with their writing, she carefully explains how to make and bind a book with outstanding results! ISBN 1-880892-22-7. Check school supply catalogs.

Art: Adding Detail to Story

In *Night of the Moonjellies,* there are a number of details you can learn about the story by looking at the pictures. These details are not mentioned in the text. (The details include: what the boat's cabin looks like inside, a sign that says marina and another sign with the prices of the food, a sign that says diving and fishing charts, a starfish and sea gulls, and the inside details of the boy's grandmother's house, etc.) Talk about the ways a illustrator's detail can help tell much more of the story than is covered in the story text. Have your older student try writing and illustrating a story, or perhaps writing and illustrating a magazine or newspaper type article with this idea in mind.

In addition, the umbrellas that the boy cranks up are not pictured on the page with the text that describes them. See if your student notices that the boy explains his chore before there is any illustration to accompany the text. Point out the illustration on the page that describes the boy and his grandma eating a quick lunch. Remind him that *those* are the umbrellas the boy is responsible for putting up and down!

Art: Viewpoint

The picture on the page where the boy gets his paper hat is drawn from a low viewpoint, as if the artist was sitting on the floor. Look at the cash register and notice how high the little boy looks on the stool. Try sitting on the floor and see how counters, desks, etc., would look if you drew them from that viewpoint. An artist-illustrator gets to choose a different viewpoint for each picture. Sometimes he will draw a picture from high up looking down on his subject, as in the pictures from *The Glorious Flight*. We call this an aerial view, or a flying "bird's eye view", like in the picture from *Moonjellies* where the boy is running with the broom and pan at the outdoor restaurant. We look down on his activity.

To vary the point of view in the illustrations of a book creates variety and makes the pictures more interesting. Many of the pictures for *Moonjellies* are from a low viewpoint (perhaps to show life from the seven year old's perspective), but some are not. Look for other examples of viewpoint in the illustrations of this story.

Remind your student that like this illustrator he can choose the viewpoint for each picture he illustrates. What viewpoint he chooses to use will depend on the message and information he desires to impart with his drawings and illustrations.

Art: Light and Dark

Find the pictures that corresponds to the text,"When the last customers left...." Hold that place in the book, and find the picture where the boy is filling the catsup container. Now flip back and forth between the two pictures. Note the effect of darkness in one and the lighter rendering of the other. Ask your student how the artist accomplished this effect. (One way is that Shasha has used dark blues in the first picture and light, bright blues in the second. Darkness is not made with black but rather subtle dark shades of blue.) Be looking for other examples of artists illustrating darkness. Note the colors they use to express dark scenes in paintings, books and magazines. (Artists rarely use pure black pigments in painting. Pen and black ink, and charcoal obviously utilize black.)

Art: Warm Palette

Grandma starts down the pier and stops at the boat. Look at the picture where the fisherman waves. The darkening blue sky gives a feeling of coolness to the night air. Grandma then says, "Let's go in and keep warm." Turn the page and experience the warmth (you can almost feel it!) of the deep orange and yellow colors. This reminds us of the warm red-orange glow of the fire reflecting off the face of Mako in *A Pair of Red Clogs*. Yellows, oranges, and reds (the colors of the sun and of fire) symbolize warmth. These colors are used by artists to help us see and virtually *feel* the heat. Remind your student that when he wants to show warmth in one of his pictures (either of actual heat like a campfire or a warmth of emotion like a loving family scene) he might want to make use of warm colors.

Math: Learning About Money

Night of the Moonjellies provides a chance to introduce the topic of money. Depending where your student is in his studies you could explain the names of the coins and bills. (Let him see real money, touch it, and notice all the differences in color, weight, etc., of the coins, and the different pictures on the bills). You may decide that it is time to explain coin equivalents, such as five pennies in a nickel, etc.

Making change is another a topic that goes well with this story of a small business. With your student fix hotdogs or sandwiches. Pretend to sell them to each other. (You will need to decide beforehand how much to charge. Ask your student how much they cost to make? What will happen if you sell the hotdogs for that price? It's best to remember to add a reasonable profit!) Then roll-play paying each other for them, and make the correct change.

Science: Moonjellyfish

Moonjellies are the most common jellyfish. They are disk-shaped, white or bluish marine animals, and are found along the Atlantic and Pacific coasts. Talk about the fact that the little boy knows that what he finds is alive because he puts it in a bag and adds seawater. What would happen if he had carried it to the restaurant without the water? What might have happened if he had added fresh water? Discuss the fact that the animals that live in water, need water to survive. Those animals that live in salt water need *salt* water, and those that live in fresh water (non-salty rivers, lakes, streams and ponds) need *fresh* water to live.

Science: Biome - Aquatic

A biome is the distinctive group of plants and animals that live in a particular geographic region defined by climate. Scientists loosely recognize the categories of different Aquatic Biomes. In this story we see or read about: starfish, sea gulls, jellyfish, clams, and lobsters. Draw a picture of life by the sea and include some of the animals, plants and birds that might be there. If there is great interest, find books at the library about the sea and oceans. For your older interested student try Amanda Bennett's *Unit Study Adventures: Oceans*. This valuable resource is loaded with information and ways to enjoy researching this fascinating topic. Check school supply catalogs.

Title:	Stopping By Woods on a Snowy Evening
Author:	Robert Frost
Illustrator:	Susan Jeffers illustrates this famous poem with sensitivity and beauty.
Copyright:	1978 (Jeffer's illustrated edition)
Summary:	A counterpoint of verse and illustration draws the reader gently into a winter night.

Note: This is not a complete lesson because it does not cover Social Studies, or Math and Science in any detail. It is a short lesson meant to be used with the Review Week plans beginning on p. 120. However, Frost's excellent verse and Susan Jeffers engaging illustrations are too good to be missed! It is included as lesson on poetry and for variety. Find this book at your library in the juvenile section. (In some libraries it may be shelved in the juvenile section of poetry.)

Language: Poet - Robert Frost

Robert Frost might be the most popular American poet of his time. He was born in 1874 and died two years after reading one of his poems at the inauguration of John F. Kennedy in 1961! His poems are associated with New England and are about common people, working people, country people and the nature around them. With your student, explore other Frost poems.(There are complete collections of his works at the library.) Try reading *Blueberries*, a story poem of boys picking blueberries, or read *Mending the Wall,* or *A Time to Talk.* Your young student will enjoy just hearing the wonderful sounds of the words in these poems, and you can discuss the messages of the poems with your older student.

Language: What Makes a Poem?

Poetry is as varied as the poets who write it. Robert Frost said, "Poetry is the kind of thing poets write." However, poetry does have certain characteristics. Poetry appeals to the reader's emotions. It often gives a sharp picture (mind's-eye *image*) of the subject. Poets use certain devices in their work including: repetition, rhythm, sometimes rhyme, personification, metaphoric language, alliteration (the repetitive consonant sounds in a line of poetry ("silver slivers shine in the sun"), onomatopoeia, and hyperbole (exaggeration--"he climbed near the sun" [pron. hi-purr-bow-lee]). These literary devices can be found in prose too, but you *expect* a poet to make greater use of them.

If a *book's* author makes much use of these techniques, he is said to have written "poetic prose". Many of the sentences in *Grandfather's Journey* are written with a poetic style even though *Grandfather's Journey* is not a poem.

Stopping By Woods On A Snowy Evening is a poem. Robert Frost has made good use of the various poetic devices, as the reader expects he would.

Language: Poetry - Alliteration

Alliteration, (pron. uh-lit-ter-ay-shun) is the repetitive consonant sound in the lines of poetry. Usually it is the initial, beginning sound, but not always. For instance: "silver slivers shine in the sun." The letter "s" at the ends of the word slivers is also alliterative. The "s" sound (not the letter "s") is alliterative. "Smooth shiny cent...", has three alliterative "s" sounds, yet not every word begins with the same letter.

There are examples of alliteration in *Stopping by Woods on a Snowy Evening:*

"the woods are lovely dark and deep"

"The only other sound's the sweep"

For your younger student it is probably enough to simply draw his attention to the "sound" of alliteration. He'll enjoy the repetitive sounds and begin to notice them in other books and poems that he hears. For your slightly older student, you may want to encourage him to try writing alliterative sentences by himself. If you feel that he needs help, you may want to begin by creating together a long list of words with the same beginning sound. Let him select several of those words and create a sentence with them. As he understands the concept he may choose to use alliteration in his writing and in his poetry.

Language: Rhyme and Rhyme Scheme

Frost's poem was originally set (as opposed to the line per page format of this book edition) in four stanzas of four lines each (called quatrains). You **name** a rhyme scheme by giving the lines with the same ending sound the same letter:

"Whose woods these are I think I know	**A**
His house is in the village though;	**A**
He will not see me stopping here	**B**
To watch his woods fill up with snow."	**A**

Thus, this poem has a rhyme scheme of **AABA** (except for the last stanza where all four ending words rhyme; deep, keep, sleep, sleep).

To introduce your older student to rhyme scheme just point out the patterns of the the ending lines. Children love the sound of rhyme, as evidenced by the popularity of Dr. Seuss, and poems from A. A. Milne of *Winnie the Pooh* fame, as well as many others. For an older student, let him try his own poem, duplicating the rhythm and rhyme scheme of the above stanza.

Also, with the poem set in stanzas, you will notice the ending word of *each third* line is the rhyming sound for the *following* stanza. "*Here,*" in stanza one, becomes the rhyming sound in "*queer, near and year,*" in stanza two, etc.

Language: Literary Device - Repetition

The ending of Frost's poem is a repetitive line: "*And miles to go before I sleep*". Repetition emphasizes the thought, and deepens the meaning.

Language: Reading Poetry to Children

Reading a lot of poetry to **young children** helps them develop an ear for interesting sounds and rhythms, increasing their literary appreciation in years to come. Some excellent books of poems for reading together are:

Now We Are Six	A. A. Milne
When We Were Very Young	A. A. Milne
The World of Christopher Robin	A.A. Milne (This is a volume of the above two titles combined.)
Favorite Poems, Old and New	Edited. by Helen Ferris
The Moon's The North Wind's Cooky	Edited. Susan Russo
Joyful Noise (Poems for Two Voices)	Paul Fleischman (Probably for Fourth grade and up; *absolutely* delightful!)
Sing a Song of Popcorn	Scholastic, Inc., edited by Beatrice Schenk de Regniers (This is also published under the title *Poems Children Will Sit Still For.*) Ages 3-10.

Art: Medium and Style

Susan Jeffers has used pencil, and pen and ink to fashion an experience in the snowy woods. Her naturalistic style (trees look like actual types of trees; the details of nature are carefully preserved) and her restrained touches of color add to the impression of a dusky winter evening.

Find the color (other than shades of grey) on each page. Ask your student what the artist was doing with her use of color. Notice exactly *what* is colored in each picture and think about what she was trying to accomplish with this use of color. (Perhaps she has separated the woods and woodland creatures from the man and his kind. You might infer this, as the houses in the village have some color too.) Can you think of other reasons the artist may have had?

Remind your student that artists choose carefully where to put color. They have particular reasons for deciding whether or not to use color, and if they do, what color expresses their message and represents their ideas. As your student progresses in his art work, he will have the same opportunity to make choices.

Notice the woodland creatures and how alive they look. Even the dried grasses and flowers are recognizable species that grow at the edge of the woods. In the picture opposite the line "*The woods are lovely, dark and deep,*" animals are hiding in the woods. See if your student can find seven animals. (a mouse, two deer, a blue jay, two rabbits, and a squirrel)*

There are obviously other animals you can't see in the picture you just studied, because if you turn two pages you see a great many animals coming out of the woods to the man's gift of food. Notice the how Jeffers portrays the cautious tendencies of animals by causing the reader to wait a page or two before the large group of animals comes out to eat. Susan Jeffers knows her subjects and draws them well, even to the timing and sequence of her pictures.

*There are other pictures with hidden animals in this book.

Art: Integrating Illustrations With Text

Susan Jeffers has illustrated Frost's poem, capturing the poet's awe and wonder at the beautiful scene before him. Look at the pictures that accompany the lines "*the only other sound's the sweep of easy wind and downy flake.*" These pictures poignantly display the man's vulnerability.. We see him in Jeffers' drawings (as the poet probably intended) unashamedly appreciating the snowy scene. The man enjoys the beautiful scene even to the point of "childlikeness" as he makes a snow angel! Ask your student to look at these pictures and ask him if he thinks the man is enjoying the snow. What could the man be thinking?"

Yet, Susan Jeffers has accomplished something else. Besides faithfully rendering the poet's words and feelings, she has also added her own story in her drawings. Had she done the latter without accomplishing the former, her work would not be true to the poem. If you read the poem carefully, you will see that there is no mention of a man making a snow angel, nor of a man feeding the animals, nor of the man's relatives. Yet, Jeffers, without harming the integrity of Frost's poem has included her elements as a sort of artistic counterpoint melody to his poem. The result is lovely and carries two stories, one in the text of the poem, woven together with the other in the illustrations.

Jeffers said of her work on this project, "I worked on the illustrations every day for six months, but I never tired of the poem." After reading it together with your student for five days in a row, it will be a part of *your* shared experiences. And you will be glad you were allowed to experience with the man, his time alone in a beautiful woods. With the last line and the last picture, the man disappears into the swirling snow. Do you wish you could follow him?

Art: Viewpoint

Jeffers' drawings are all done from the bird's-eye or aerial view. This makes the reader of the story feel as if he is sitting on a branch of the tree looking down on the scene. The one exception (variation) to this is the picture corresponding with the line "*Between the woods and frozen lake--the darkest evening of the year.*" In this picture, the reader sees from the animal's viewpoint and looks *up* slightly, at the man digging for something in the back of his sleigh. How has Susan Jeffers accomplished the task of making the reader feel as if he is looking up? (She elevates the man high up into the corner of the picture and places the animal subject (through whose eyes the reader is looking, in the lower opposite corner). She also, makes the man smaller than the animal, so the man looks higher up and far away.)

Art: Mood

The mood of Frost's poem is quiet, like the quiet of freshly-fallen snow that muffles the sounds around it. The mood of Jeffers' drawings corresponds with the poet's writings. The illustrations are as quiet and lovely as Frost's words and the woods themselves. There is calmness in the fact that the man is alone. This is a solitary experience. Can your student think of a special time when he saw or appreciated something when there was no one else around?

Art: Detail and History

Discuss the familiar song *Jingle Bells*. In the song, the "jingle bells" are like the bells in Jeffers' illustrations and the "one horse open sleigh" is like the sleigh in Jeffer's illustrations. Seeing a picture of the subject of this famous song can make a difference in your student's understanding. Then, he can understand what a sleigh looks like and won't be confused as one child once was, thinking the words to the song were "a one horse soap and sleigh." If you have an opportunity, take a sleigh ride with your student. Farmers and stables sometimes offer such rides if you don't happen to have a friend with a sleigh! Of course some snow is good too. For areas of the country without snowfall you might enjoy finding some children's movies that show snow storms and sleigh rides. (There's a sleigh ride in the video *Anne of Avonlea*, produced by Kevin Sulluvan, Wonderworks. There may be similar scenes in *Heidi*, etc.)

Also, notice the beauty in the detail of the snowflakes on the page with the line "*...and downy flake.*" Contrast this detail with the last picture of the snow flurry where no single flake is visible.

Don't forget to enjoy the curled up fox on the title page. He looks like he's keeping warm. Many times the pictures on the title page are overlooked because the reader tends to turn directly to the story's beginning. Some pictures on title pages are quite beautiful and some give information about the coming story. Remind your student to begin reading at the title page. (Actually noticing the covers of the book, any pictures on the inside covers, or book jackets is also beneficial to the enjoyment and understanding of the story.)

Memorizing Poetry

Stopping By Woods on a Snowy Evening is a good poem to memorize (for the teacher or older student) because of the gentle way the words sound next to one another. The peace and tranquility of the poem is comforting and the appreciation of the beauty of nature is inspiring, while the repetition at the end nearly lulls the reader to sleep.

Math: Flash Cards

Make math flash cards or concept cards using animals or animal tracks to tie them to the story. There are suggestions for making flash cards in the How to Use Five In A Row, Math section pp. 10-11.

Science: Animal Tracks

In several pictures of *Stopping By Woods on a Snowy Evening* you can see tracks of the man and his horse. Near the end, you can also see the tracks of the sleigh as it glides away. Open the book and look for these tracks.

Let your student know that during times of snow, one can often see animal tracks as well. Maybe he has already noticed cat, dog, or bird tracks on snowy days. There are other animals that he might be able to detect with some help. (Even in the cities or suburbs, one can often see the tracks of squirrels, rabbits, and mice. In the country the list grows: raccoons, skunks, turtles [in the summer!], deer, and many more.) Even if your student lives where there is no snow, let him know he can usually find animal tracks in dust, or mud. This is especially true at the edges of creeks and rivers, etc. Studying the tracks of animals in the snow or in dust or mud, both in winter and in summer, can be an exciting adventure. Two excellent adult books to help the teacher with such adventures are:

A Guide to Animal Tracking and Behavior   Donald and Lillian Stokes
A Guide to Nature In Winter   Donald Stokes

A book that your student would enjoy on this subject is:

Crinkleroot's Book of Animal Tracking   Jim Arnosky

Review Week

If you wish, take a week to review the books, authors, and illustrators you've studied in *Five in a Row* Volume 1. Recall which titles were award winners. Figure out which book is the oldest, and which book was written the most recently. Discuss the stories you and your student particularly liked and which characters or ideas were your favorites. If you do not own the books, use the colorful story disks to bring back memories of the stories.

Look again at the art work and review the elements of art that you have learned. If you have kept an illustrated chart of art definitions and elements, review it now. Examine your student's art work for the semester. Point out examples you feel are outstanding. Let him see how much he has learned!

If your student has kept a notebook, leaf through it with him, recalling various projects and reviewing concepts in Social Studies, Geography, Science, and Math.

In Language, review the elements of a story and literary devices. If you have kept an illustrated chart of these items, use it for a comprehensive review. Look over the exercises, stories, and poems that your student has written. Point out specific work that was creative or excellent.

Review the vocabulary words using your illustrated list or file box. Recall the stories in which they appeared and practice using them.

See how many story disks your student can correctly place on the Literature Map. If you have studied the continents and oceans, practice placing those, too. Review the lessons in finding directions, and compass points on the map. Remember with him the directions he discovered relating to his home and neighborhood.

Thank you for using *Five in a Row* Volume 1. I hope you enjoyed using it with your student. If so, you'll want to continue with Volume II, which includes stories that can be used any time, but will fit particularly well into the spring semester. And please tell a friend about *Five in a Row*!

Sample Semester Planning Calendar

This is merely a sample semester schedule. It ties *Cranberry Thanksgiving* to Thanksgiving, etc. Feel free to use the titles in any order you wish. *Storm in the Night* can be used as an alternate title if you find one you don't care to use, or pulled out of sequence and used when you'll likely experience thunderstorms during the last week of August. If a certain title is unavailable at your local library this week, simply switch with another title!

	August — Storm in the Night *(optional)*

September	September	September	September
The Story About Ping	Lentil	Madeline	A Pair of Red Clogs

October	October	October	October
The Rag Coat	Who Owns the Sun?	Mike Mulligan	The Glorious Flight

November	November	November	November
How to Make an Apple Pie	Grandfather's Journey	Cranberry Thanksgiving	Another Celebrated Dancing Bear

December	December	December	December
Papa Piccolo	Very Last First Time	Clown of God	*(Holiday Vacation?)*

January	January	January	January
(Holiday Vacation?)	Katy and the Big Snow	Night of the Moonjellies	Stopping by Woods & Review

Sample Lesson Planning Sheet

Title:
Who Owns the Sun?

Author:
Stacy Chbosky*

Illustrator:
Stacy Chbosky

Note: *Winner of 1987
"Written & Illustrated
by .. " Award

Monday	Tuesday	Wednesday	Thursday	Friday
Social Studies	Language Arts	Art	Math	Science
Read story through, then:	Read story through, then:	Read story through, then:	Read story through, then:	Read story through, then:
Family Relationship Talk about Father and Son:	List Making	Discuss the artist who was 14 years old when she wrote and illustrated this book!	Counting	Discuss Five Senses: smell hearing touch feeling sight
Father's wisdom	List the qualities of Big Jim from the reading		Count pickets of fence pp. 7 and 21	
Son believes him and admires him	(What was Big Jim like?)	Her paintings are simple and strong. Show a pic-ture with fine details to point out the contrastof Chbosky'smore simple art style. Filled with strength and emotion.	Count stars on p. 9	from the story and find them on p. 7, etc.
Son's labor of love p.21	List words on paper as you remember them together		Count flowers on p. 17	
Son finds out the hard truth of slavery (how would you feel if you were not free?)	Print word with symbol picture beside it:	How does she do this? (Action and Color)	Count tree stumps on p. 25	Seasons Spring; story begins Summer: story ends
	BIG HANDS!	What colors are on the pages? New colors: Chartruese and mauve	Use story motif to make cards for addition of twos (2+3) Put answers on back. (5)	Name the characteristics of Spring and Summer
Son knows father can't control everything	(Add to the list as we remember more through the week. Be on the look-out for Big Jim characteristics)	Do the pictures of the sun make you feel warm? What colors did she use for this? Note also shadows and bright light.		Memory Game:
Going on with and making something out of his life.				What did Mother pack in Father's lunch?

Sample Lesson Planning Page: *Who Owns the Sun* has twenty suggested lessons in the lesson portion of this manual. The sample planning sheet above shows twelve ideas that *could* be chosen for a one-week study. You are free to choose *any* of the twenty lesson ideas and keep track of your choices by noting them on the reproducible, blank Lesson Planning Sheet (Following page). For more ideas on making the best use of your *Five in a Row* curriculum, be sure to read the *How to Use Five in a Row* section beginning on p. 5.

Blank Lesson Planning Sheet (Reproducible)

	Monday	Tuesday	Wednesday	Thursday	Friday
Title:					
Author:	Read story through, then:	Read story through, then:	Read story through, then:	Read story through, then:	Read story through, then:
Illustrator:					

Body Action Sheet
(*A Pair of Red Clogs*, p. 29)

These skeletal "stick" figures were made by laying tracing paper over some of the illustrated figures in the story *A Pair of Red Clogs*. Take tracing paper and trace them. Now lay your traced paper over your story book and try to find the figures that match. Trace some other figures from the story. When you come to clothing, just imagine where the body lines would actually be, according to the position of the figure.

Quilt Pattern
(The Rag Coat, p. 34)

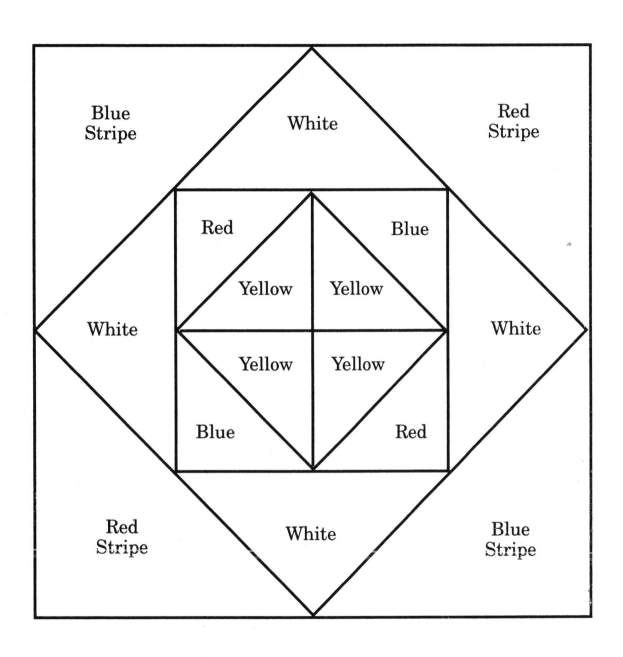

Joseph's Coat of Many Colors

Pinwheel Pattern
(Mike Mulligan and His Steam Shovel, p.46)

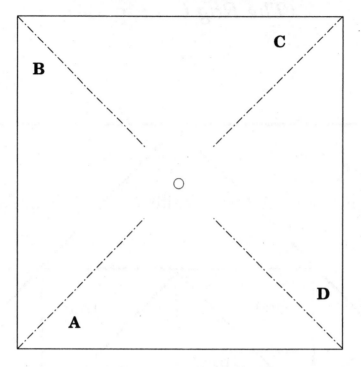

Reproduce this pattern or use a square piece of paper. Cut on dotted lines. (Do *not* cut all the way to the center dot!) Fold lettered corners to center and glue. Allow it to dry. Insert a straight pin through center of pinwheel and into a pencil eraser, so that the pinwheel spins on the pin. Find a teapot with a good spout which produces a solid "stream" of steam. Boil some water until the teapot steams. Hold the pinwheel near the steam adjusting carefully until the steam begins to turn the pinwheel. Yes, steam has "energy" to power your pinwheel and to do other types of work as well!

***Note-* Be careful! Steam can cause serious burns!!**

We Gather Together

Netherlands Folk Hymn

1626

We gath - er to - geth - er to ask the Lord's bless - ing. He
chas - tens and has - tens His will to make known; The wick - ed op -
ress - ing now cease from dis - tress - ing; Sing prais - es to His
name, He for - gets not His own. A - men.

Verse 2

Beside us to guide us our God with us joining
Ordaining, maintaining His Kingdom Divine.
So from the beginning the fight we were winning
Thou, Lord, was at our side all glory be Thine!

Verse 3

We all do extol Thee our leader triumphant
And pray that Thou still our defender will be.
Let Thy congregation escape tribulation
Thy name be ever praised O, Lord, make us free.

(Cranberry Thanksgiving - p. 65)

Domes for a Russian Skyline
(Another Celebrated Dancing Bear, p.75)

Reproduce or trace these domes and have your student color, cut and paste them along the top of a blank page of paper, grouping some of them together. Now draw building beneath them for a Russian style skyline.

Color Wheels- Primary, Secondary and Complementary

(Papa Piccolo, pp. 79-80)

Primary Colors

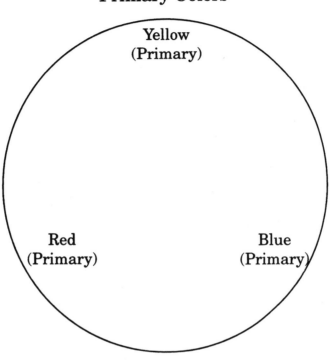

Secondary Colors

Complementary Colors

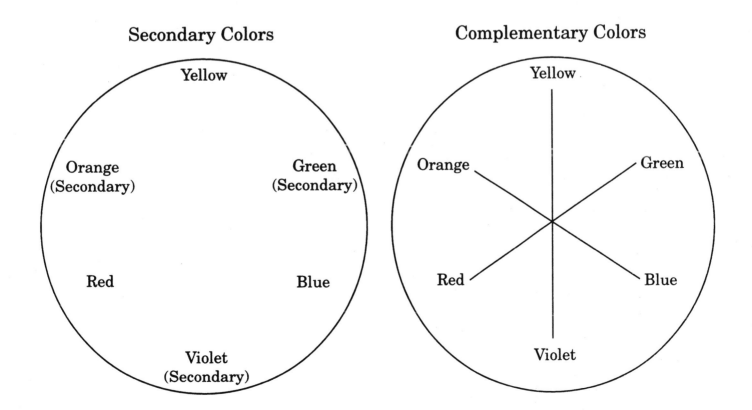

Literary Glossary

Literary Devices

Alliteration A succession of similar *sounds* (not letters) can occur at the beginning of words or internally. "Susie's galos*hes* made spli*shes* and splo*shes*..."

Apostrophe A way of addressing an absent person or some inanimate thing not usually spoken to. "*O, Moon!...*"

Hyperbole An overstatement or exaggeration: "*I've told you a thousand times!*"

Irony An event or outcome which is opposite what would naturally be expected: "*It was an irony of fate that the girl arrived just as her date left.*"

Mood The feelings a work of literature brings to the reader: sad, for boding, boyant, etc., derived from the particular descriptive words chosen by the writer.

Onomatopoeia Representing a thing or action by a word that imitates the sound associated with it: *zoom, ping, ding-dong, buzz.*

Personification Where a thing, animal or abstract truth is made human, given human characteristics: "*The Man in the moon.*"

Repetition The repeating of certain words, phrases, or ideas throughout a story or poem: "And I will take you home with me
Yes, I will take you home with me.

Rhyme Words where the ending *sounds* (not necessarily the letters) are the same: "Don't blame *me,*
go and *see...*"

Symbolism Writing that suggests more than the literal meaning. "*The innocent girl wore a white dress.*" (White being a symbol of purity.)

Elements of a Story

Characters   A person, animal, or thing (wind, for example) that inhabits a story.

Point of view   Who narrates (tells) the story:

    First Person–using I, me, etc.
    Third Person–using he, she, they.

The point of view is usually the same throughout a short story but you will find some stories where it changes. Ask," who is telling this story?" Is the story told through only one character's view? (first person) Or through the overall view of the narrator? (third person)

Mood   The feelings a story stirs in the reader: calm, happy, sad, fearful, etc. The mood of a story can change, e.g., from an ominous beginning to a happy ending, etc. Sometimes there is a pervasive mood throughout a story such as wistfulness, etc.

Plot   The action, the story line. Includes:

Conflict	the problem of the story
Rising Action	the growing excitement
Climax	the high point of excitement
Denouement	the resolution or final outcome

Theme   The general idea or insight revealed in the story. The *heart and soul* of the story.

Setting   Where does the story take place: geography, town, a room, etc.? The time frame for the story: an hour, a day, a certain year or period of years, a season, etc.

Style   Someone once said, "Style is the *clothes* the words wear." In other words, how they are dressed-what *fashion* of words and sentence structure a writer uses to *outfit* his story. Many famous writers have distinctive styles. You can often tell by reading only a few paragraphs who wrote a passage. You would say, "Oh, that story sounds like it was written by ...."

Bibliography of *Five in a Row* Titles

The Story About Ping, Marjorie Flack, ISBN 0-590-75747-4, Viking Press.

Lentil, Robert McCloskey, ISBN 0-14050.287-4, Puffin Books.

Madeline, Ludwig Bemelmans, ISBN 0-670-44580-0, Viking Press.

A Pair of Red Clogs, Masako Matsuno, ISBN 0-399-20796-1 (pbk.), Philomel Books, New York.

The Rag Coat, Lauren Mills, ISBN 0-316-57407-4, Little Brown & Co., Boston.

Who Owns the Sun?, Stacy Chbosky, ISBN 0-933849-14-1 (lib. bdg.), Landmark Editions, Inc., Kansas City, Mo.

Mike Mulligan and His Steam Shovel, Virginia Lee Burton, ISBN:0-395-16961-5 Reinforced Ed., ISBN 0-39525939-8 Sandpiper Ed., Houghton Mifflin Co., Boston.

The Glorious Flight, Alice and Martin Provensen, ISBN 0-14-050729-9, Puffin Books, New York.

How to Make an Apple Pie and See the World, Marjorie Priceman, ISBN:0-679-83705-1 (trade), ISBN 0-679-93705-6 (lib. bdg.), Alfred A. Knopf, New York.

Grandfather's Journey, Allen Say, ISBN 0-395-57035-2, Houghton Mifflin Co., Boston.

Cranberry Thanksgiving, Wende and Harry Devlin, ISBN 0-8193-0498-0 (trade), ISBN 0-8193-0499-9 (lib. bdg.), Parents' Magazine Press, New York.

Another Celebrated Dancing Bear, Gladys Scheffrin-Falk, ISBN 0-684-19164-4, Charles Scribner's Sons, New York.

Papa Piccolo, Carol Talley, ISBN 1-55942-028-6, Marsh Media, Kansas City, Mo.

Very Last First Time, Jan Andrews, ISBN 0-689-50388-1, Atheneum- Macmillan Publishing. Co., New York.

Clown of God, Tomie dePaola, ISBN 0-15-219175-5, ISBN: 0-15-618192-4 (pbk.), Harcourt Brace Jovanovich.

Storm in the Night, Mary Stolz, ISBN 0-06-025912-4, ISBN:0-06-025913-2
(lib. bdg.), ISBN:0-06-443256-4 (pbk.), Harper Trophy, div. Harper Collins.

Katie and the Big Snow, Virginia Lee Burton, ISBN 0-395-18155-0 (reinforced ed.),
ISBN 0-395-18562-9 (pbk.), Houghton Mifflin Co., Boston.

Night of the Moonjellies, Mark Shasha, ISBN 0-671-69282-7, Simon & Shuster,
New York.

Stopping By Woods On a Snowy Evening, Robert Frost (Susan Jeffers'
Illustrations), ISBN 0-525-40115-6, E.P. Dutton Publisher., New York.

Finding the Books

In our experience, a "typical" library may actually have 20-25 of the 55 *Five in a Row* titles within their own system. The rest they will have to obtain through Inter-library loan (ILL). We've also observed that juvenile fiction is frequently mis-shelved because children examine books at random while mother makes her selections, replacing the books on the shelves *wherever is convenient*! The result is that even though the computer may indicate a given volume is "available," you may have a very difficult time locating it on the shelf.

We've found the most time-effective way to utilize the library system is to get a stack of library request cards from your librarian. If you own all 3 volumes of *Five in a Row*, you'll need 55 cards. Then, take the hour needed to fill them *all* out and put a rubber band around them, placing them in your purse or organizer. Keep them with you. Whenever you go to the library, simply turn in two or three cards for any titles that are not on the shelf and let *them* do the searching. *They* will locate the mis-shelved book when the computer indicates it's available. *They* will flag the computer to automatically "hold" the title for you when another library patron returns the book. *They* will request books via ILL and hold them for you when they arrive.

(Note- Some library systems and some librarians are still resistant to doing ILL, but that is changing. A recent article by one of the foremost authorities on library science in the world suggested that while ILL was practically unknown a few years ago, it is common practice today in most libraries. She went on to say that ILL will continue to grow as libraries inter-connect their computerized catalogs. She concluded by saying that a good librarian today should *never* tell a patron, *"I'm sorry but we don't have that book,"* without quickly adding, *"but I'll be happy to locate a copy for you!"*)

As your local library collects your requested titles they will call you every week or two to let you know another book or two is being held for you. Then, when you go to check out your new acquisitions, turn in two or three more cards and let them begin the search/request/hold cycle all over again. You will discover a comfortable rhythm of swinging by the library every two weeks or so and picking up your next title or two. It can be very painless!

Another note on the subject. One of the benefits of requesting a title is that often a library will eventually purchase the book if it's requested often enough. If the library comes up empty handed on a particular title, keep requesting it every few weeks. Encourage your friends to request it too! You'd be surprised how many wonderful books end up in the system that way.

A personal anecdote: A dear friend who began reviewing *Five in a Row* several years ago obtained *Who Owns the Sun?* via ILL. When she returned it suggested the librarian consider purchasing a copy for the local library. The busy librarian quickly brushed her aside saying, *"I'm sorry, but we've already spent our budget for this year; it's out of the question."* Our friend simply opened the book and began reading it aloud to the librarian right at the check-out desk! Before she was halfway through, the librarian was wiping away tears as she listened to the poignant story, and by the time our friend finished reading, the librarian grabbed the book from her saying, *"I'm going to take $15 from our office supply budget and order this book immediately!"*

Sadly, many of the most wonderful books being written today, as well as the marvelous classics like *The Story About Ping* are being supplanted on limited library shelf space by books of far less merit. The library system is designed to respond to patron usage and requests. They buy and maintain what the most people are reading. One of our more subtle opportunities is to bless our communities with wholesome, solid books by requesting them, sharing them with local librarians, or even donating a copy of a special title from time to time. Our libraries are what we make them!

One final note on the titles of *Five in a Row*. We're well aware that several of the books are difficult to locate and several others are currently out of print for those who wish to *purchase* them. While we struggled with this issue, in the final analysis we concluded that we wanted to offer the very *best* of the more than 5000 children's books we've explored and examined. In the three volumes, we've supplied 55 lesson plans; 55 weeks of unit study to keep you going through a calendar year. (The joy of reading wonderful books and discussing what you've read can be a year-round activity.)

We know that even if you keep going year-round, you're only likely to actually use 43-45 titles because of vacation breaks, Christmas breaks, etc. The "extra" titles are provided so that if there are several books you cannot locate or which are unavailable through your local library, you'll still have more than enough material to keep your young ones learning for a full year. *But,* for those who are willing to leave no stone unturned in their search for all 55 titles, we're sure you'll be blessed and rewarded for your trouble. Some of the most difficult titles to find are some of the richest!

The cost of *Five in a Row* is just slightly more than $1 per unit study. Even if you only locate two thirds of the titles successfully, you'll still be getting wonderful, inspired unit studies for less than $1.50 each. And in the meantime, keep on the lookout for other titles, by trading with friends, having relatives check their libraries, requesting again and again locally, exploring used bookstores and flea markets, etc.

In the final analysis, we've tried to give you the very "best of the best" from the more than 5,000 children's books Jane has explored in the hopes that each one will be a present tense joy and a lifetime friend for both you and your children. God bless you and your children as you set out on the wonderful adventure of learning with *Five in a Row*.

Integrating *Five in a Row* with Additional Curriculum

For teaching three, four and some five-year-olds, you will find *Five in a Row* to be an exciting and complete curriculum. Once you make the decision that your student is ready to begin phonics, reading and mathematics you will want to supplement your *Five in a Row* curriculum with additional materials.

Thereare many wonderful products available to help you teach phonics/reading and mathematics. You will find helpful descriptions of available products in homeschool curriculum catalogs. You may also want to make plans to see and review these materials first hand by planning to attend a homeschool convention or curriculum fair in your area. Most of these events occur between March and July each year.

Once you integrate your new reading/phonics and mathematics curricula with *Five in a Row* your teaching day may look something like this:

Morning
Math instruction
Five in a Row (read the story aloud and discuss one of the five subject areas)
Lunch (Nap?)

Afternoon
Phonics/Reading instruction

Or perhaps you'll want to do phonics and mathematics in the morning and save your *Five in a Row* until after lunch as a sort of *reward* for the morning's work. Other mothers prefer to do *all* their work in the morning when their student is *fresh*. Arrange your teaching day in whatever way works best for you and your student. Don't be afraid to change or rearrange your schedule to provide variety, flexibility or to try new schedules until you find what works best for you. There is *no* right or wrong way to do it! Some mothers like to create a chart for their schedule. Perhaps your schedule might look like this:

Monday	Tuesday	Wednesday	Thursday	Friday
Math	Math	Math	Math*	Math
Phonics	Phonics	Phonics	Phonics	Phonics
FIAR Social Studies	FIAR Language Arts	FIAR Art	FIAR Applied Math	FIAR Science

*You may or may not want to omit your math curriculum lesson on Thursday and concentrate on the *Five in a Row* math lesson instead. We believe it's important *not* to skip the *Five in a Row* math lesson however, because *it* teaches your student how mathematics is applied in life all around him including measuring, telling time, counting money, sewing, building, etc. This lesson time will stimulate math curiosity and motivate your student to learn math!

Finally, if you are using *Five in a Row* with older students, third grade and older, consider adding brief grammar and punctuation lessons. Workbooks containing these lessons are available through curriculum catalogs, teacher's stores, bookstores and even at your local Wal-Mart! Some of these books are quite good and cost less than $3.00. One series that we've found useful (and there are many) is the *Brighter Child Series*. One book is entitled *English Grammar and Writing for Grade 3*. ISBN 1 56189-083-9 published by American Education Publishing, 150 E.Wilson Bridge Rd., Suite 145, Columbus, OH 43085. Of course there are other books available for grade four, five, etc. These simple, affordable booklets can supplement *Five in a Row* for your older students, supplying the needed sequential learning that's appropriate for language arts.

For Science and Social Studies, you might consider having your older student do additional, self-directed research and reporting on several of the hundreds of topics you will encounter while doing *Five in a Row*.

By enriching *Five in a Row* using advanced, student-directed research and reporting and by supplementing the curriculum with additional work in mathematics, grammar and punctuation, you'll find *Five in a Row* can serve as the educational base from which you build for children from pre-school through elementary school.

MASTER INDEX

Social Studies Index

Social Studies Geography

Social Studies Relationships

Language Index

Art Index

Math Index

Science Index

References to Supplemental Books Mentioned in the Text:

A Guide to Animal Tracking and Behavior,

Other Products from Five in a Row

Before Five in a Row by Jane Claire Lambert- This treasury of learning ideas was created for children ages 2-4. Enjoy exploring 24 wonderful children's books while building a warm and solid foundation for the learning years just around the corner. ISBN 1-888659-04-1 $24.95

Five in a Row Volume 1 by Jane Claire Lambert- First published in 1994, the new, revised, second edition is now available. Volume 1 contains 19 unit studies built around 19 of the very best children's books ever printed. Each unit takes five days to complete. Created primarily for children ages 4-8 but don't be afraid to include other ages too! ISBN 1-888659-00-9 $19.95

Five in a Row Volume 2 by Jane Claire Lambert- An all new, revised, second edition is now available. Volume 2 explores 21 more outstanding children's books. Each unit takes five days to complete. Created for ages 4-8. ISBN 1-888659-01-7 $24.95

Five in a Row Volume 3 by Jane Claire Lambert- An all new, revised, second edition is now available. Volume 3 explores 15 additional outstanding children's books. Each unit takes five days to complete. Created for ages 4-8. ISBN 1-888659-02-5 $19.95

Five in a Row Christian Character and Bible Study Supplement by Jane Claire Lambert- This wonderful resource teaches hundreds of non-denominational Bible lessons and concepts using the first three volumes of Five in a Row. Teach your children about obeying parents, kindness, generosity, good stewardship, forgiveness and more. Ages 4-8. ISBN 1-888659-03-3 $17.95

Laminated Full Color Story Disks by Jane Claire Lambert- Each volume of Five in a Row contains black and white story disks. Use these little half-dollar sized drawings to teach children geography by attaching them to your own large, world map as you explore each new Five in a Row story. Just cut out the disks, color and laminate them. However, we offer this optional set of already colored, laminated disks for those who prefer to save the time needed to prepare their own. These disks are printed in full color and heat laminated- ready to use. One set of these disks covers all three volumes of Five in a Row. Beautiful and ready to enjoy! $15.00

Beyond Five in a Row Volume 1 by Becky Jane Lambert- This exciting new curriculum is the answer for all those moms who have asked, "What do I do <u>after</u> Five in a Row?" You'll find the same creative, thought-provoking activities and lesson ideas you've come to expect from Five in a Row using outstanding chapter books for older children. Volume 1 will keep your students busy for a full semester with history, geography, science, language arts, fine arts and issues of human relationship. Each unit also includes numerous essay questions, career path investigations, optional internet sites to explore and much more. Volume 1 requires The Boxcar Children, Homer Price, and the Childhood of Famous American Series biographies of Thomas A. Edison- Young Inventor and Betsy Ross- Designer of Our Flag. Created for ages 8-12. ISBN 1-888659-05-X $24.95

Beyond Five in a Row Bible Christian Character and Bible Supplement Volume 1 by Becky Jane Lambert- This companion volume to Beyond Five in a Row Volume 1 provides a rich selection of the wonderful Bible links and strong character lessons you've come to expect from Five in a Row. This valuable supplement teaches traditional Christian values such as honoring parents, forgiveness, generosity, etc. Easy to use! ISBN 1-888659-06-8 $ 9.95

Beyond Five in a Row Volume 2 by Becky Jane Lambert. Requires Sarah Plain and Tall, The Story of George Washington Carver, Skylark, and Helen Keller. ISBN 1-888659-07-6 $24.95

Beyond Five in a Row Bible Christian Character and Bible Supplement Volume 2 by Becky Jane Lambert. This is the companion volume to Beyond Five in a Row Volume 2. ISBN 1-888659-08-4 $9.95

*<u>NEW</u>- Beyond Five in a Row Volume 3 by Becky Jane Lambert. Requires Neil Armstrong- Young Flyer, The Cricket in Times Square, Marie Curie- and the Discovery of Radium, and The Saturdays. ISBN 1-888659-09-2 $24.95

*<u>NEW</u>- Beyond Five in a Row Bible Christian Character and Bible Supplement Volume 3 by Becky Jane Lambert. This is the companion volume to Beyond Five in a Row Volume 2. ISBN 1-888659-10-6 $9.95

*<u>NEW</u>- The Five in a Row Cookbook by Becky Jane Lambert. This companion volume to Five in a Row (Volumes 1-3) and Beyond Five in a Row (Volumes 1-2) provides complete recipes and menus to complement each story you study. You'll enjoy the opportunity to wrap up each unit with a family meal, a time of celebration, and the opportunity for your students to share their achievements. You'll also appreciate the scrapbook area for photos, notes and homeschool memories. ISBN 1-888659-11-4 $22.95

Name_____ Date_____

Shipping Address_____

City_____ State_____ Zip_____ Country_____

Phone_____ E-Mail_____

Check - MasterCard - Visa (Circle One)   Credit Card Expiration Date_____

Credit Card Number_____

Item Description	Qty.	Price	Total
Before Five in a Row Ages 2-4		$ 24.95	
Five in a Row - Volume 1 Ages 4-8		$ 19.95	
Five in a Row - Volume 2 Ages 4-8		$ 24.95	
Five in a Row - Volume 3 Ages 4-8		$ 19.95	
• Buy All 3 Volumes of *Five in a Row* and Save 10%		$ 58.50	
Five in a Row Christian Character and Bible Supplement		$ 17.95	
Laminated Full Color *Five in a Row* Story Disks for Geography		$ 15.00	
Five in a Row Cookbook		$ 22.95	
Beyond Five in a Row - Volume 1 Ages 8-12		$ 24.95	
Beyond Five in a Row - Volume 2 Ages 8-12		$ 24.95	
Beyond Five in a Row - Volume 3 Ages 8-12		$ 24.95	
• Buy All 3 Volumes of *Beyond Five in a Row* and Save 10%		$ 67.50	
Beyond Five in a Row Christian Bible Supplement for Volume 1		$ 9.95	
Beyond Five in a Row Christian Bible Supplement for Volume 2		$ 9.95	
Beyond Five in a Row Christian Bible Supplement for Volume 3		$ 9.95	
• Buy All 3 Volumes of *Beyond Christian Bible Supp.* and Save 10%		$ 26.95	
Audio tape: *Getting the Most out of Before FIAR* - Jane Lambert		$ 6.00	
Audio tape: *Getting the Most out of Five in a Row* - Steve Lambert		$ 6.00	
Audio tape: *Getting the Most out of Beyond FIAR* - Becky Lambert		$ 6.00	
Audio tape: *Teaching Art for Early Learners* - Jane Lambert		$ 6.00	
Audio tape: *Combining Multiple Ages Simultaneously* - Steve Lambert		$ 6.00	
Audio tape: *Five in a Row and the Internet* - Panel Discussion		$ 6.00	
Audio tape: *Beginning the Homeschool Journey* - Steve Lambert		$ 6.00	
Audio tape: *Finishing the Homeschool Race* - Steve Lambert		$ 6.00	
Audio tape: *You CAN Do Unit Study* - Steve Lambert		$ 6.00	
Audio tape: *Creating Your Own 1-Room Schoolhouse* - Steve Lambert		$ 6.00	
• Buy Any Six Audio Tapes and Save 10%		$ 32.40	

Make Check Payable To:
Five in a Row
P. O. Box 707
Grandview, MO 64030-0707

Merchandise Total	
Missouri Residents Add 7.10%	
Shipping & Handling Charges	$5.95
Total	